THE OLMSTED STORY

THE OLMSTED STORY

A BRIEF HISTORY OF OLMSTED FALLS & OLMSTED TOWNSHIP

BRUCE BANKS & JIM WALLACE

THE History PRESS

Published by The History Press
Charleston, SC 29403
www.historypress.net

Front cover: The Village Green has served as a public park in Olmsted Falls since the 1830s. Today, it includes a gazebo dedicated to former mayor William Mahoney, a grindstone from a nearby quarry bearing a memorial plaque for local servicemen who died in World War II and the Schoolhouse Pavilion, which is on the site of the Union Schoolhouse (1873–1960), designed to somewhat resemble the old school and to hold the school bell. *Photo by Jim Wallace.*

Back cover: *Left*: Union Schoolhouse, 1873–1960. *Right*: Schoolhouse pavilion, designed to somewhat resemble the old school. *Photo by Bruce Banks.*

First published 2010

Manufactured in the United States

ISBN 978.1.59629.898.9

Library of Congress Cataloging-in-Publication Data

Banks, Bruce, 1942-
The Olmsted story : a brief history of Olmsted Falls and Olmsted Township / Bruce Banks and Jim Wallace.
p. cm.
Includes bibliographical references.
ISBN 978-1-59629-898-9
1. Olmsted Falls (Ohio)--History. 2. Olmsted (Ohio)--History. I. Wallace, Jim, 1954 Aug. 29- II. Title.
F499.O55B36 2010
977.1'31--dc22
2010022983

CONTENTS

OLMSTED CHRONOLOGY

1795	Aaron Olmsted and other Connecticut men bid for Township 6, Range 15 land.
1807	Land sale consummated for then–Plum Creek Township.
1809	Calvin and Lemuel Hoadley build mill at West View.
1814	James Geer farms land in township, then called Kingston.
1815	Geer moves family into township.
	Stearns family arrives.
1816	Geer and David Stearns build Butternut Ridge Road.
1819	First wedding (Harvey Hartson and Eunice Parker) held at Geer's home.
	First frame house built by Hoadleys (Columbia and Butternut).
1820	Lemuel Hoadley builds mills near Cedar Point.
1820	TeGrotenhuis House (Nobottom and Columbia) built by John Adams and Maria Hoadley.
1821	First person (Isaac Scales) is buried at Butternut Ridge Cemetery.
1823	Civil township called Lenox is formed.
1825	Township is divided between Middleburgh and Ridgeville Townships.
1827	Lenox Township is put back together.
1827	Waterous Usher builds sawmill on Plum Creek near current Usher Road.
1828	Orson Spencer suggests renaming township "Olmsted."
1829	Township changes name to Olmsted.

1830 Wooden schoolhouse built on land (Village Green) donated by Barnum family.
1831 Fitch family arrives.
1832 Lemuel Hoadley builds sawmill at Plum Creek.
1833 Peter and Asenath Kidney arrive.
1833 Charles Hyde Olmsted ships Oxcart Library books to Olmsted.
1834 Newton Loomis arrives.
1835 First Congregational Church organized.
1836 Lemuel Hoadley and son-in-law John Barnum build house (Water and Main).
1840 (or earlier) Rocky River Seminary built (Lewis Road).
1845 Post office name "Norris Falls" changes to "Olmsted Falls."
1845 Church (Columbia and Sprague) built by Hoadleys.
1848 Lester, Philo and Myron Bradford establish paint factory on Minnie Creek.
1848 Congregational church built.
1849 Cleveland, Columbus and Cincinnati Railroad opens through West View.
1853 Methodist Church built.
1853 Lake Shore & Michigan Southern Railroad opens through Olmsted.
1853 Home built (8008 Columbia) with Bradford bricks.
1854 Stone livery stable (Orchard and Mill) built.
1856 Olmsted Falls incorporates as a village.
1856 Father Louis Filiere founds St. Mary's of the Falls Church.
1857 Plum Creek hamlet annexed to Olmsted Falls.
1858 St. Mary's church built on site of current Olmsted Community Church.
1858 Seminary building moves to Columbia and Mill Streets to become Grand Pacific Hotel.
1864 Gib Doolittle builds first Water Street Bridge.
1870 Luther Barnum opens quarry in Olmsted Falls.
1870 Colonel H.N. Whitbeck operates mill in Olmsted Falls.
1870 Sam and Joseph Lay build broom and brush factory.
1873 St. Mary's of the Falls moves down Columbia Street.
1873 Union Schoolhouse built (Village Green).
1876 Ed Damp buys Whitbeck's mill.
1876 Olmsted Falls Depot opens.
1882 Thomas Chambers acquires Hoadleys' Mill.

1883 Severe flood damages mills and bridges.
1883 Town hall opens.
1886 Cleveland Stone Company acquires quarries.
1887 Grand Army of the Republic Post #643 forms.
1888 Railroad spur to quarry built in Olmsted Falls.
Philip Simmerer joins Joe Peltz in hardware/drugstore business.
1893 Peltz and Simmerer move hardware/drugstore into hotel.
1903 First Odd Fellows Hall burns down.
1906 Ed Damp sells mill.
1908 North Olmsted incorporates as village.
1908 Olmsted Falls abolishes saloons.
1909 Second Odd Fellows Hall moves when railroad widens bridge.
1913 Severe flood damages mills and bridges.
1913 Jim Scroggie builds second Water Street Bridge.
1915 Village and township school districts merge.
1916 Consolidated school built.
1917 Olmsted Community Church forms through merger.
1917 Olmsted Falls PTA forms.
1920 Chambers's mill ceases operation.
1924 Depositors Bank Building constructed.
1927 West View incorporates as a village.
1939 Township Hall built.
1942 New Olmsted Falls Town Hall opens.
1948 Fire destroys St. Mary's church building.
1948 Railroad passenger service to Olmsted Falls ends.
1950 New St. Mary's of the Falls Church is dedicated.
1954 Falls Elementary School opens.
1954 Railroad freight delivery to Olmsted Falls ends.
1955 Library moves to N.P. Loomis House on Main Street.
1956 Olmsted Community Church Fellowship Hall completed.
1958 Fitch Elementary School opens.
1960 Olmsted Community Church Sanctuary opens.
1960 Union Schoolhouse torn down.
1961 Lenox Elementary School opens.
1967 Fire destroys Barnum's grocery.
1968 New high school opens.
1971 Olmsted Falls and West View merge.
1972 Olmsted Falls becomes a city.
1987 Berea annexes Bagley Road Corridor.

1989 The Renaissance opens.
1990 Clint Williams begins Grand Pacific Junction restoration.
1992 New Falls-Lenox Primary building links existing Falls and Lenox schools.
1996 New middle school completed.
1997 1916 school is sold.
1998 Charles A. Harding Memorial Bridge dedicated.
2000 Bulldogs win state football championship.
2001 City offices and police department move to 1916 school building.
2009 New intermediate school opens.
2009 Bulldogs win state volleyball championship.

TWO OLMSTEDS, ONE COMMUNITY

In Olmsted Falls and Olmsted Township, the past is present, still there in three dimensions, even if the fourth dimension—time—keeps moving on. And the past is a present, a gift that keeps giving to current and future generations.

History is preserved and on display in Olmsted, from entire buildings to grooves carved in stones.

"Olmsted Falls is one of the oldest villages in Northern Ohio; it is likewise one of the prettiest and most romantic," a correspondent for the *Berea Advertiser* wrote in November 1897. "The natural scenery along the rapids in the river is picturesque and worthy of the artist's pencil and brush."

If that writer could return to twenty-first-century Olmsted Falls, he or she would notice many changes—from automobiles on the streets to airplanes overhead to cellphones in people's hands. But that person could still recognize many remaining nineteenth-century buildings, including dozens of homes and shops. The time traveler also could find the same picturesque views along Rocky River and Plum Creek. If anything, those views have become even prettier and more romantic because they are now protected in a municipal park rather than lying in an industrial zone of quarries and mills.

Being tucked into a southwestern corner of Cuyahoga County helped Olmsted retain many small-town attributes. Growth that spread out from Cleveland, especially after World War II, was slower in reaching Olmsted. Other suburbs got big shopping centers and industry. More of Olmsted remained undisturbed long enough to be preserved.

But Olmsted came close to losing much of its historic charm. In the 1980s, plans emerged to build a bank at Columbia Road and Mill Street.

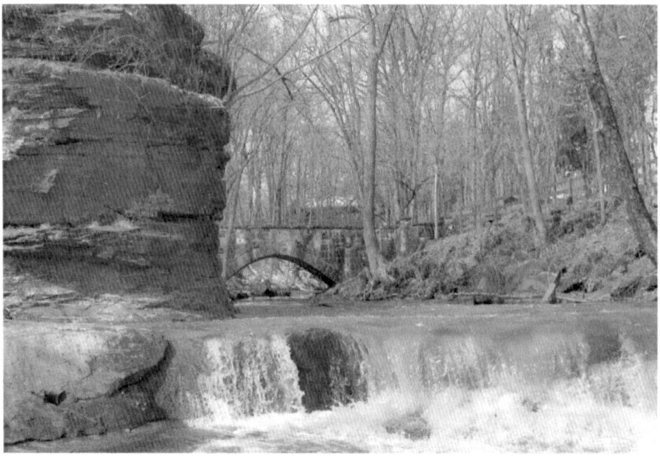

The mouth of Plum Creek was the site of an early mill, which dammed water at Inscription Rock (left). The WPA built the stone bridge in the 1930s. *Photo by Jim Wallace.*

It would have displaced one of the oldest buildings in town, now known as the Grand Pacific Hotel. If it had been lost, nearby buildings might not have been saved. Fortunately, that deal fell through, and real estate company owner Clint Williams found new uses for those old buildings as Grand Pacific Junction.

Olmsted Falls and Olmsted Township are really one community in two. They share a school system, a post office (zip code 44138), a telephone exchange (235), a public library, community life and rich history.

Only in local government are they separate: Olmsted Falls has been a municipality since 1856 with a mayor and council. Olmsted Township is under the authority of three trustees, a system from Ohio's early nineteenth-century government organization.

Many attempts have been made to unite them. None has been successful so far, even though township government is anachronistic in Ohio's most urbanized county. Municipalities have replaced almost all of the county's original twenty-one townships. Neighboring cities have nibbled away at parts of Olmsted Township. But the survival of ten of its original twenty-five square miles almost two centuries after its creation is another example of holding onto the past in Olmsted.

Throughout Olmsted, roads named Fitch, Lewis, Stearns, Schady, Usher and Cook are lasting testaments to settlers who cleared land for farms and homes. There are fewer farms today, but many more homes, for a combined population of almost nineteen thousand.

Not all is ideal in Olmsted. Frequent trains and low-flying airplanes disturb the peace. Residents would welcome controlled light industrial and

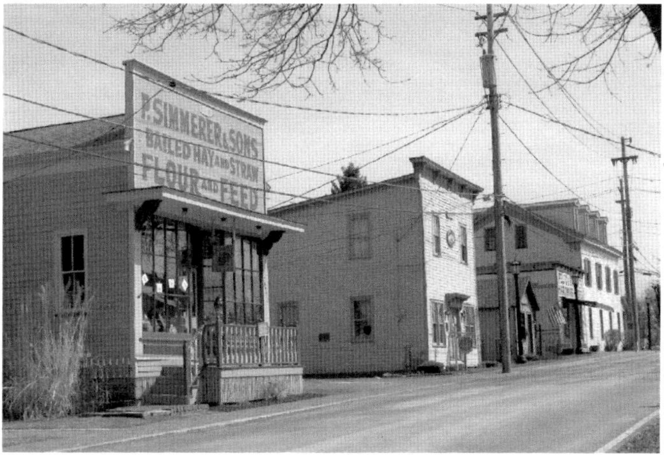

The Granary, Warehouse, Olde Jail and Grand Pacific Hotel are a few of the restored nineteenth-century buildings at Grand Pacific Junction. *Photo by Jim Wallace.*

commercial development to reduce the burden of having among the area's highest residential property taxes to support schools and other services. But those schools score high academically and athletically.

Nevertheless, the best qualities of small-town American life are found in Olmsted. People still line streets for parades, flock to festivals like the annual Olmsted Heritage Days in the summer and Falls Day in the Park in the autumn and follow the high school sports teams, the Bulldogs.

Les Roberts captured that essence in his 2008 mystery novel, *King of the Holly Hop*. He wrote that Olmsted Falls "drips charm" much like such other quaint towns in northeastern Ohio as Hudson and Chagrin Falls.

"It boasts historic homes and a delightful business district called Grand Pacific Junction, with a delicious bakery, interesting and unusual shops, and an amazing French restaurant, Bistro du Beaujolais," Roberts wrote. "About a block away is the local library, and the waterfall just behind it gave the town its name. Olmsted Falls shivers and vibrates as trains pass directly through downtown blowing their ear-shattering whistles, but otherwise the village feels rural, quiet, and almost turn of the twentieth century."

In 1941, Eugene Segal wrote in the *Cleveland Press*, "Olmsted Falls is a village that knows what it wants to be. By choice, it is unindustrious, small, tranquil and slow-moving." Today, Olmsted Falls is a city; Olmsted Township is big enough to be one. Though they are not as slow-moving as they once were, they remain more tranquil than other communities. They know that what they want to be is not much different than what they are, which is still a reflection of all they have been for two centuries.

"A" IS NOT OK IN OLMSTED

Olmsted has had different names, including Kingston, Plum Creek and Lenox, but "Olmstead" was never one of them. Yet a myth has persisted that the name once had an "a" that was dropped at some unspecified time.

For example, Olmsted Township's official website in 2010 provided the following explanation:

> *In 1829, the community agreed to name itself after Charles Olmstead in exchange for his library, said to be the first west of the Alleghenies. In the course of time the "A" was dropped from the name and the name and this area was known as Olmsted Township.*

The Cuyahoga County Public Library, the Ohio Historical Society, history books, newspaper articles and many other sources have offered similar explanations. But they are wrong.

The first misspelling of Olmsted occurred in the original courthouse documents of land acquisition by Aaron Olmsted. The records (now in the Trumbull County Courthouse) show that the recorder sometimes spelled the name with an "a" and sometimes without one.

Perhaps Crisfield Johnson also was to blame. His 1879 *History of Cuyahoga County* has much useful information about the community, including several stories that came directly from early settlers. But he apparently never checked the official records of Olmsted Township or Olmsted Falls, which had the correct spelling. He simply spelled the name "Olmstead."

Almost ninety years later, in his very detailed 1966 history, *Township 6, Range 15*, Walter F. Holzworth wrote unquestioningly that the family for whom the township was named was "Olmstead."

Records say otherwise. For example, the Historical Society of Olmsted Falls has three letters written by Aaron Olmsted, the Connecticut sea captain who won the right to buy a huge section of the township in 1795. In his signature on each letter, there is no "a" in Olmsted. The same is true for a signed portrait of him.

Further proof is found in books in a display case at the North Olmsted Library. They are from the Oxcart Library, which Aaron's son, Charles, sent to the community. One book was written by a relative, Denison Olmsted. Another book, *Lay of an Irish Harp*, was signed by another of Aaron's sons, Aaron Franklin Olmsted. In each case, no "a" appears in Olmsted. In addition, early township records show that the name was "Olmsted."

One reason the myth might have persisted is that it seemed plausible, especially in a suburb of Cleveland. Moses Cleaveland, who founded the city in 1796, had an extra "a" in his name. The city's first newspaper, the *Cleveland Advertiser*, reportedly took the first "a" out of the name in 1830,

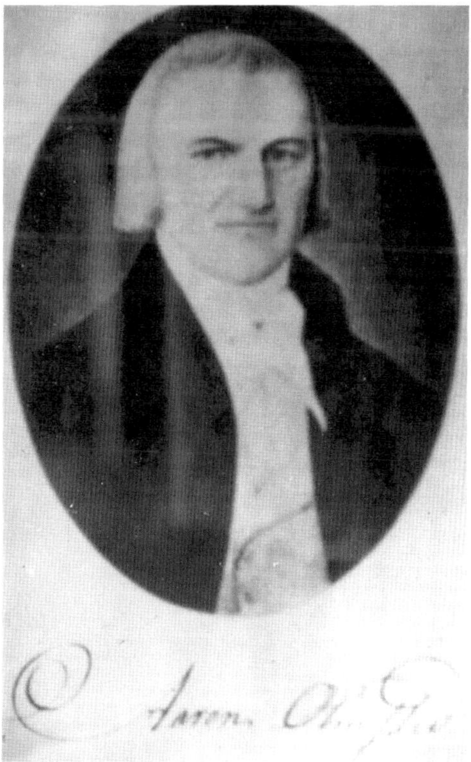

Aaron Olmsted signed his surname with no "a" in it.

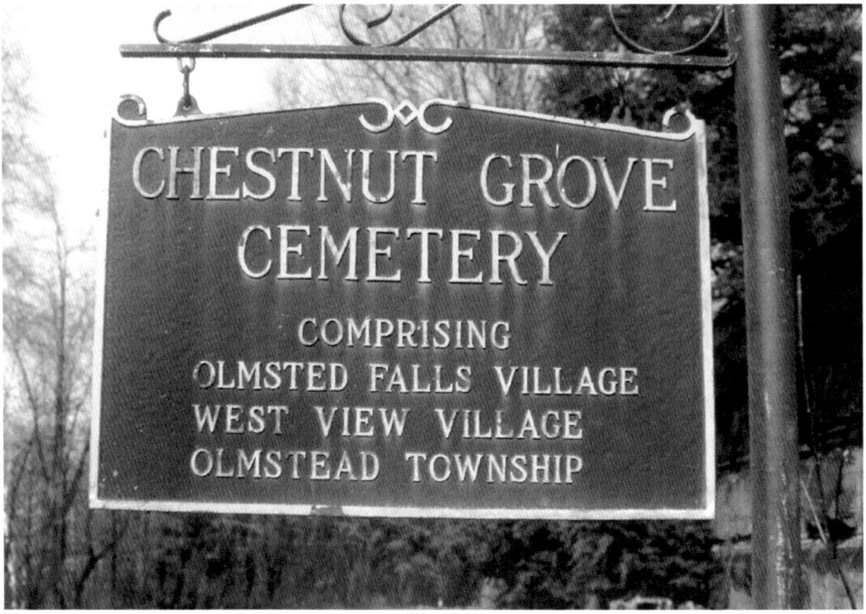

Even in the twentieth century, Olmsted was sometimes misspelled. *Photo by Bruce Banks.*

because the original version was too long to fit on the paper's masthead, and the new spelling stuck. Another story contends that a spelling error occurred on the original map made by surveyors. No matter which story is correct, it was well known in northeastern Ohio that Cleveland had dropped an "a" from its founder's name. Thus, it would seem logical that the same could have happened with Olmsted.

But unlike the Cleveland story, the erroneous story about Olmsted's spelling change doesn't include a date for when it occurred or a reason for its occurrence. That's because there never was a change.

It's likely that many people simply misspelled the name because it is so similar to "homestead." Indeed, that misspelling often pops up on printed sales receipts from stores in North Olmsted, Olmsted Falls and Olmsted Township, as well as in other printed matter. Both spellings of the name are oddly exhibited at the original Chestnut Grove Cemetery in a decades-old sign that refers to "Olmsted Falls Village" and "Olmstead Township."

Changing a metal sign like that is not so easy, but the myth that Olmsted once had an "a" should be retired.

EARLY SETTLEMENT

1795–1849

History generally praises the pioneers, the trailblazers, the people who go first—Leif Ericson, Christopher Columbus, Ferdinand Magellan, Charles Lindbergh and Neil Armstrong. But the first settlers of European heritage in the township that became Olmsted were latecomers. They arrived almost two decades after New Englanders started building homes in northeastern Ohio.

Until 1800, Connecticut claimed the strip of northeastern Ohio land, extending 120 miles west from Pennsylvania, known as the Western Reserve. Connecticut sold most of that land in 1795 for $1.2 million at forty cents an acre to the Connecticut Land Company. The company divided the territory into townships of twenty-five square miles, five miles long on each side.

The company sold land in what was called officially Township 6, Range 15—unofficially, Plum Creek Township—in a "punchbowl draft," a type of auction in which parties would bid for land without seeing it first. In that lottery, a sea captain named Aaron Olmsted of East Hartford, Connecticut, was among several buyers who pulled out slip number forty-five. That gave him the opportunity to purchase almost half of the township on its northern side for about $1.80 an acre.

Other purchasers of township land included: David Tuttle, who paid $685.36; Ashbel King and others, who paid $2,500.00; Joseph Lynde, who paid $800.00; John Worthington, who paid $1,600.00; Daniel Phoenix, who paid $2,952.68; Horace Perry, who paid $1,222.73; and Thomas James Douglas, who paid $2,000.00. Others who bought parts of the township were listed as: Rising and Pierce, who paid $200.00, and King and Kendall, who paid $1,223.00.

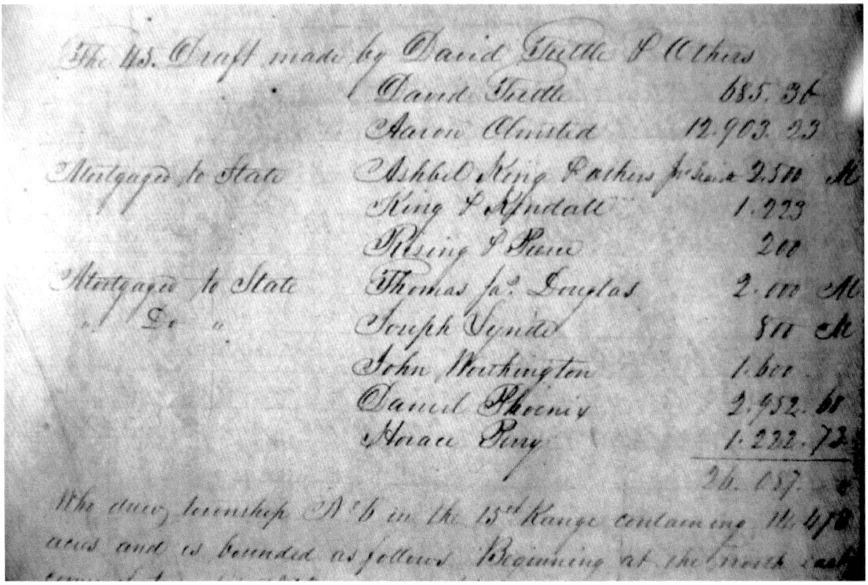

The W.S. Draft made by David Tuttle & Others
David Tuttle 685.36
Aaron Olmsted 12.903.23
Mortgaged to State Ashbel King & others 2.500
King & Lyndall 1.223
Rising & Pease 200
Mortgaged to State Thomas Jas. Douglas 2.100
Do " Joseph Lyndal 800
John Worthington 1.600
Daniel Phoenix 2.952.61
Horace Perry 1.222.72
26.087
The above township No 6 in the 15th Range containing 16.470
acres and is bounded as follows Beginning at the north east

Aaron Olmsted was among several Connecticut men who bought parts of the township.

Olmsted was forty-two years old when his certificates of purchase were signed on September 5, 1795. Unfortunately for him, he died on September 9, 1806, at age fifty-three without seeing his land. It took until 1807 for the sale to be consummated for $12,903.23 by his heirs—widow, Mary Hyde Olmsted, and sons, Horace Bigelow Olmsted, Aaron Franklin Olmsted and Charles Hyde Olmsted. They sold some of the property to settlers.

Moses Cleaveland, leader of a Connecticut Land Company team, founded Cleveland in 1796. Settlement throughout northeastern Ohio soon followed, but Township 6, Range 15, was bypassed. The first settlers arrived in Columbia Township to the south in 1807, in Middleburgh Township to the east and Ridgeville Township to the west in 1809 and in Dover Township to the north in 1810.

GEER'S CLEARING

In 1814, Columbia Township resident James Geer cleared a small plot in the southeastern corner of the future Olmsted Township. As Crisfield Johnson wrote in his 1879 history of Cuyahoga County, Geer planted corn on the land "and raised such a crop as he could among the trees." Although Olmsted Falls and Olmsted Township claim they were founded in 1814, it was not until the next spring that Geer built a small log house on the land and moved his family there. Thus, in 1815, the Geers became the first permanent residents of the township.

Geer's son, Calvin, was seven at the time. Many years later, he told Johnson about "wild beasts" that appeared at the edge of their clearing and of his father's killing of a bear on the bank of Rocky River. "Mr. Geer's first shot broke the animal's back, but such was his size and vitality that it took three more balls to kill him," Johnson wrote.

In addition to farming, Geer made shoes for a living. Historian Walter Holzworth wrote in 1966 that Geer "set up a rude tannery, using sap troughs for vats. He pulverized oak bark for tannic acid and followed the shoe maker trade which he learned from his wife, whose first husband was a shoe maker in Waterbury, Connecticut."

Mrs. Geer is credited with weaving the first cloth in the area using wild hemp her husband found near Rocky River. Holzworth wrote that James Geer "made a loom and weaving rack and his talented help mate spun and wove about 15 yards of cloth and colored it with buttered bark."

The Geers also were responsible for two other firsts in the township. Their two-year-old daughter, Julia, became the first child to be buried there. And their home became the site of the first wedding in 1819, when Mrs. Geer's daughter, Eunice Parker, married Harry Hartson, who lived in the northern part of the township.

More New Englanders Arrive

Other settlers also came to the township in 1815. Elijah Stearns and his sons, David and Alvah Stearns, arrived from Vermont and bought 1,002 acres for two dollars each along Butternut Ridge. Johnson wrote that Elijah Stearns "had a large family of boys, and was desirous to obtain an extensive tract of land for their use." His other four sons—Vespacian, Elliot, Elijah and Asaph—joined David and Alvah in settling the land. They were the first of many settlers from Vermont. In the early years, many settlers came from Vermont and Connecticut, a trend that no doubt contributed to the New England appearance that Olmsted acquired.

Favorable opinions about Ohio from these early settlers might have influenced fellow New Englanders to join them, but an atmospheric abnormality in 1816 also could have played a role. It was known as "the year without a summer," and "eighteen hundred froze to death." Snow fell in New England in May and June. Crop-damaging frosts occurred in July and August. The cause was unknown to the Americans and Europeans affected by the cold, but it was later determined to have been the April 5, 1815 eruption of Mount Tambora, an Indonesian volcano. It sent so much ash and sulfuric acid into the atmosphere that by 1816, significantly less solar radiation was able to get through. That summer was also cool in Ohio, although it was not as bad as in New England. So many New Englanders decided then to move to Ohio that the urge to migrate became known as "Ohio fever."

David Stearns and James Geer celebrated the Fourth of July in 1816, the fortieth anniversary of the Declaration of Independence, by clearing out a road along Butternut Ridge from Rocky River to Stearns's home. "They worked from sunrise till sunset, cutting out the saplings so as to make a passable pathway, for a distance of two miles," Johnson wrote.

In those early years, the township was called Kingston, reportedly after Ashbel King, one of the original land purchasers. But as Johnson noted, the name "had no legal validity; it was merely applied at the fancy of the proprietors to survey township number six."

One of the early settlers, Isaac Scales, came in 1818 but died in 1821. He was buried in his backyard, and that was the beginning of the Butternut Ridge Cemetery.

In 1819, Major Lemuel Hoadley moved with his family into a log cabin near there (Columbia and Butternut Ridge Roads). Soon after that, he began construction of a larger frame house. Just after the frame was completed and ready to be raised, Hoadley and his wife went away for a day, leaving their daughters, Maria and Eunice, home. Two men, carpenter James Miles and Eliot Smith, were also there, and Mrs. Scales came over. "The two girls, both enterprising, wide-awake young women, determined that they would surprise their parents by raising the new house while they were gone," Johnson wrote. "When Major and Mrs. Hoadley returned at nightfall, their eyes were greeted with the sight of a frame completely erected and ready for the clapboards, while, to their astonished inquiries, two demure young ladies answered quietly, 'Oh, we did it.'" Portions of that house, built in 1819, with original butternut wood floors, are in a house that still stands on Columbia Road just south of Butternut Ridge Road.

Streams and Ridges

Settlement of the township picked up after 1819. In those years, Hoadley and Crosby Baker built the township's first gristmill and first sawmill on the west branch of Rocky River near Cedar Point (near the current Frostville Museum). As Johnson wrote, woods were cleared "here and there in all parts of the township except the southwestern section, which was the last to be settled."

Locations along Rocky River and Plum Creek were prime spots for some early settlers who took advantage of water power. A trail along the west side of Rocky River served as the only north–south road from Butternut Ridge to the center of what became Olmsted Falls. A portion of that trail was called Bradford Road (now River Road). Many of the community's oldest homes were built there.

The other key locations for settlement were along the township's northern ridges because the land was high and well drained. After that, parcels farther south along what is now Cook Road were the choice, but settlement was much slower in the southern part of the township. As Holzworth explained it, "Here the heavily forested land, clay and soil retained excessive moisture well into May and June, and unless deep ditches were dug or drain tile was used it couldn't make good farm land."

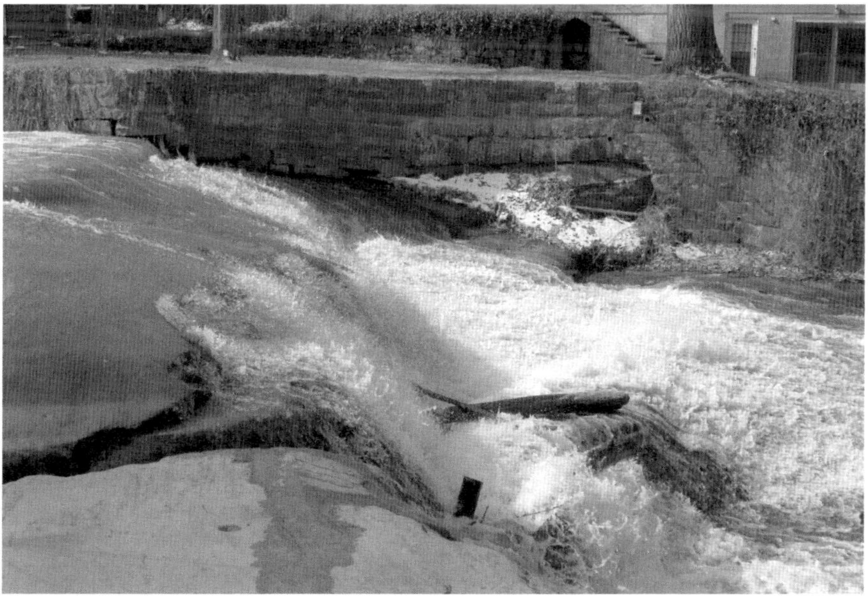

The waters of Plum Creek turned mill wheels for many years. *Photo by Jim Wallace.*

By the time settlers moved into the township, not many Native Americans were left in the area. The Erie tribe, which occupied northern Ohio as late as the 1650s, was devastated by war with the Iroquois. The Delaware and Ottawa tribes moved in after the Eries left, but wars and treaties with the United States from 1805 through 1813 drove most of them out. Some wigwams reportedly stood in the township as late as the 1820s. As Johnson wrote, "Indians frequently came and set their traps for the various fur-bearing animals which still abounded." The Indians also would come annually from Sandusky to boil sap to make sugar, he noted. But after the 1820s, the Native Americans apparently quit visiting Olmsted.

NAMING RIGHTS

In 1823, a civil township, the most basic level of local government in Ohio, was organized. Although many people had been calling it Kingston, it was named Lenox Township instead for unexplained reasons. An April 14, 1823 election selected Amos Briggs, Hosea Bradford and Watrous Usher as the first trustees, David Stearns as clerk and Isaac Frost as treasurer.

Two years later, the Ohio General Assembly decided to cut Lenox Township in half, assigning the western half to Ridgeville Township in

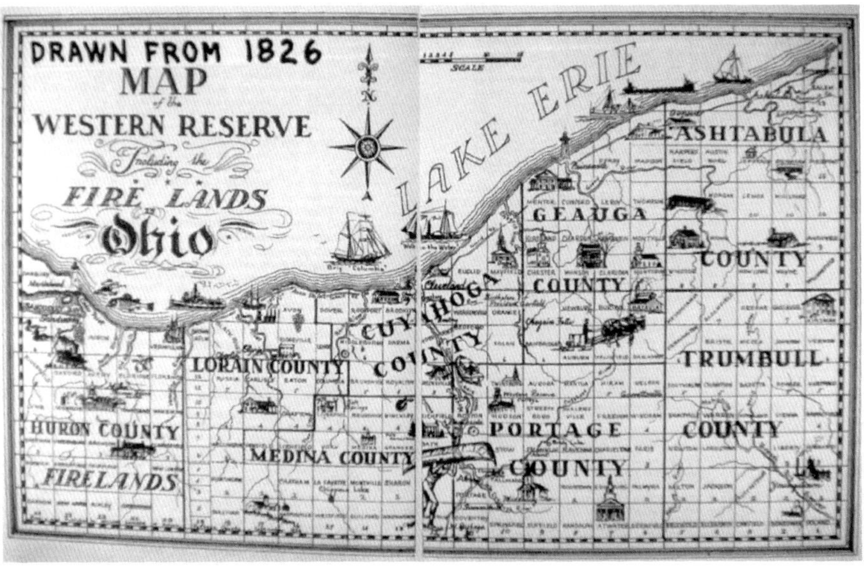

From 1825 until 1827, the state split Lenox Township between two counties.

the newly formed Lorain County and the eastern half to Middleburgh Township in Cuyahoga County. But residents were upset and persuaded legislators, on January 29, 1827, to put Lenox back together. By the township's next election that June 18, it had about four hundred residents. In addition to trustees, a clerk and a treasurer, voters elected a justice of the peace, two constables, two overseers of the poor, two fence viewers and four supervisors of highways. The township soon was divided into three school districts. Also in 1827, Usher built a sawmill along Plum Creek (near the current Usher Road).

The township might have remained Lenox, but another township in Ashtabula County had the same name. Letters sent to people in one Lenox sometimes ended up in the other. In Cuyahoga County, resident Orson Spencer got fed up and suggested renaming the township Olmsted for the family that originally owned its northern portion. Spencer sent an inquiry to Charles Hyde Olmsted about whether that would be acceptable.

Olmsted was so pleased with the proposition that he offered to send books to start a community library. The name was changed in 1829, and the first election under the name Olmsted Township occurred in 1830. Olmsted sent about 500 books, many of them religious, from Connecticut by oxcart. They were covered in heavy blue paper, but many were damaged by rain. The Oxcart Library (originally called the "Olmsted Library Company") is believed to be the first publicly owned circulating library in northeastern Ohio. Several residents divided the responsibility of caring for the books and lending them to others. (About 150 of the books have survived, many in their original blue covers. They are in a display case in the North Olmsted Library.)

Small Industry

About 1830, the area near where Plum Creek empties into the west branch of the Rocky River became a busy industrial site. First, Major Hoadley and his son-in-law, John Barnum, built a sawmill at the mouth of Plum Creek. Barnum had bought the land (including what is now the Village Green, Fortier Park and part of the Olmsted Community Church property) in 1820. Previously, Barnum had worked in Hoadley's sawmill near Cedar Point.

As Johnson wrote, soon after Barnum and Hoadley built the sawmill on Plum Creek, Barnum built a house:

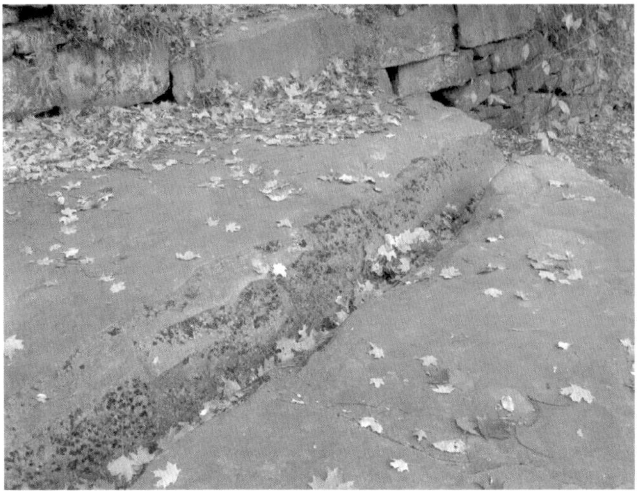

A hand-chiseled channel near the mouth of Plum Creek appears to have been a sluice for Hoadley and Barnum's mill. *Photo by Bruce Banks.*

> *He cut down a large whitewood tree near the bank of the creek, and this formed one end of his house. A few smaller logs were laid up, some saplings placed on top to support a temporary roof and the mansion was complete. However, Mr. Barnum speedily constructed a more commodious residence.*

This second house, with one and a half stories, was at what later became the corner of Water and Main Streets. (Although Barnum's son, Luther, and Luther's wife, Mary, later remodeled the house, it still stands at 25334 Water Street.)

Also in 1830, the township built a frame schoolhouse on land (now the Village Green) donated by Barnum next to his house.

Not long after Hoadley and Barnum built their sawmill, Uriah Kilpatrick built what Johnson referred to as "a little 'packet' gristmill, also on Plum Creek. Both the mill and its owner were of a slow and easy nature, and the patience of his customers was sometimes severely tried." Kilpatrick's mill lasted about a decade.

Beginning in 1831, seven Fitch brothers—Chester, Eli, Horace, Chauncey, Elisha, Daniel and Sanford—moved to the township with their wives. Like the Stearns family, the Fitches and their offspring played important roles in the development and civic life of Olmsted.

Peter Kidney, who arrived in a covered wagon in 1833 with his wife, Asenath, and family from upstate New York, built a sawmill and a small gristmill along the Rocky River, north of the mouth of Plum Creek near the trail that became Bradford Road (now River Road). Kidney used local

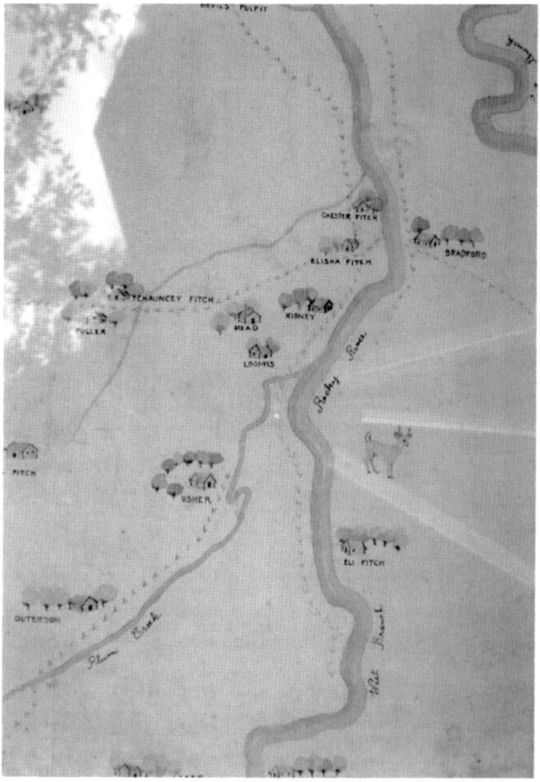

An 1834 map shows how sparsely settled the future Olmsted Falls was.

sandstone to sharpen tools and built a triphammer for making such tools.

Thus, the center of what would become Olmsted Falls was busy with mills and toolmaking in the early 1830s, but it lacked a good road. Newton P. Loomis, who moved from Connecticut to Olmsted in 1834, later told Johnson that instead of a road, there was only a path along the river. He said a main road had been "slashed out" but was not ready for use. Loomis initially made chairs but later switched to making coffins and then became a merchant.

Also about that time, William Romp built a large wood-framed building near Butternut Ridge and Rocky River (now the corner of Columbia and Cedar Point Roads) to serve as the township's first hotel. He also operated the township's first store there. This was just south of the township's first post office, established in 1829 by postmaster Elias Frost.

Churches

In the early years, residents formed a Methodist society and held worship services in homes or traveled to neighboring communities for services. According to Johnson, the township's first Sunday school was established in 1833 or 1834 on Butternut Ridge, which "was settled by a very enterprising, wide-awake set of people, and all intellectual and moral improvements found ready encouragement at their hands."

About 1835, members of three denominations—Methodist, Presbyterian and Universalist—raised funds and built the Union House of Worship. This church also was used for conducting township business, so that area was called Town House Corners. (Although Holzworth placed it at what became the corner of Lorain and Barton Roads, historians Bernice Offenberg and Dale Thomas placed it near what are now Butternut Ridge and Columbia Roads. Johnson said the location was "some two miles north of Olmsted Falls," which fits the Butternut Ridge–Columbia Road location. Holzworth seems to have confused the Union church with a church the Methodists built in 1847 at the corner of Lorain and Barton Roads. The Universalists also built a separate church in 1847 at the corner of what are now Lorain and Butternut Ridge Roads, although it was moved in 1863 to Porter Road.)

The Universalists had the largest congregation, so they contributed about half the cost. Charles Olmsted gave the church $100. The Methodists and Presbyterians came up with the rest of the funds. The congregations handled the church as a timeshare operation, or as Johnson put it, "the time which each was allowed to occupy it being in proportion to the amount subscribed." That arrangement lasted for nine years.

PANIC AND HAMLETS

Just as Olmsted was developing, the Panic of 1837 gripped the nation following a period of high speculation. It began a recession that lasted several years. On May 10, 1837, all the New York City banks stopped making payments in gold and silver coins. Unemployment ran as high as 10 percent at times, and more than 40 percent of American banks failed. According to the Ohio Historical Society, many Ohioans lost all of their savings, and many stores refused to accept currency for payment of debts. At that time, much currency was issued by banks, instead of the federal government, and not all of it was backed by gold or silver. Most northeastern Ohio banks closed. Private credit and business loans dried up. Railroad and building projects stopped.

By 1840, the population of Olmsted Township had reached 659 people. In the early 1840s, two hamlets took shape on the township's eastern side. E.S. Hamlin, a lawyer and state legislator from Lorain County, laid out one as far south as Hamlin Street (now Bagley Road) and as far north as the current Elm Street. In 1843, it had the township's second post office and was called Norris Falls, although it is not clear why. In 1845, it became Olmsted

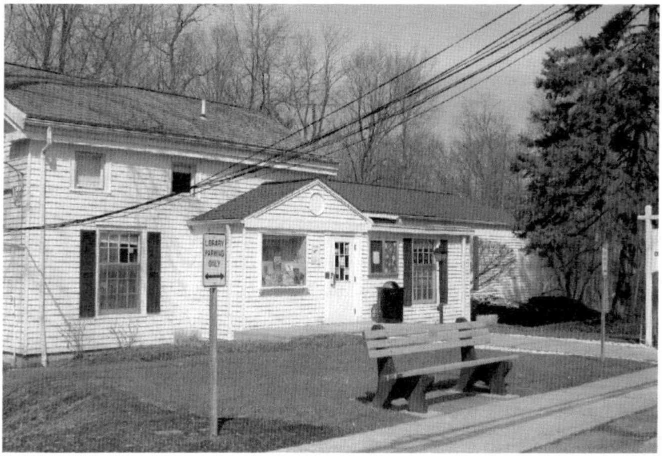

Newton Loomis's 1834 house moved twice before it became the Olmsted Falls Library. *Photo by Jim Wallace.*

Falls. Directly north was another hamlet, Plum Creek, which included the confluence of Plum Creek and Rocky River, as well as the current River Road. The western boundary ran west of the current Columbia Road. The northern boundary was the current Cook Road.

In 1843, Newton Loomis bought land from Hamlin and built a general store in Olmsted Falls. This was the beginning of his long career as a prominent merchant in the community.

In 1846, Olmsted Falls even became the home of one of the earliest newspapers in Cuyahoga County, the *True Democrat*. It was an antislavery publication owned by Hamlin, who supported the Whig Party. He moved the newspaper to Cleveland in 1848.

The Congregational church in Olmsted Falls was built in 1848 (at the current location of the Olmsted Community Church's parking lot). Members organized the church in 1835. Initially, they met in Chauncey and Nancy Mead's home. (That house still stands at 7674 Columbia Road, across from the Village Green.)

Township officials changed the place for conducting their business from Town House Corners to Olmsted Falls in 1849, according to Johnson. Later, they began meeting in the Methodist Episcopal church, built in 1853 across the street from the Congregational church. Johnson wrote that the township purchased the basement of the Methodist church in 1856 "for a town house, at a cost of two hundred and fifty dollars."

From 1840 to 1850, the population of Olmsted Township almost doubled to 1,216. As the first half of the nineteenth century ended, the township was ready for further development and incorporation of its first municipality.

BEYOND THE PIONEERS

1850–1900

The first three and a half decades of settlement in Olmsted Township established a modest little agrarian community with rudimentary dirt roads, several mills, a few churches and a few stores. By the mid-1800s, "the pioneer period had changed into the farming period," as historian Crisfield Johnson put it.

Small farm clearings grew larger. Frame houses replaced log cabins. "Pumps appeared instead of the picturesque but inconvenient well-sweeps which were previously seen in every door-yard," Johnson wrote. (A well-sweep is a lever used to raise and lower a bucket in a well. Typically, a Y-shaped tree was the fulcrum and a long log was the lever.) Many residents clustered along Butternut Ridge in the north and in the twin hamlets of Olmsted Falls and Plum Creek along the Rocky River on the eastern side of the township.

Riding the Rails

At midcentury, railroads arrived. In 1849, the Cleveland, Columbus and Cincinnati Railroad cut through the township's southeastern corner. The depot there was named West View Station. Although Olmsted Falls was small at that time, West View was smaller. Nevertheless, as Holzworth wrote in his history of Olmsted, "a small but jubilant crowd" was on hand when the first train passed through on July 1, 1850. He called it "a brass trimmed wood burning locomotive with no cowcatcher or head lights, pulling a box

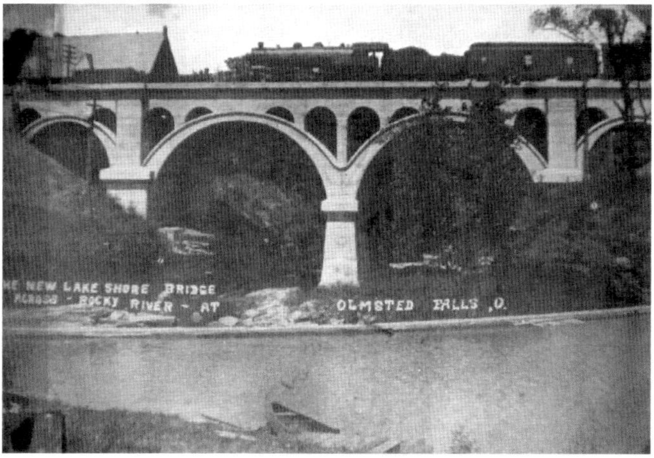

The railroad built a big bridge to cross the Rocky River in Olmsted Falls. This bridge, built in 1909, replaced the original bridge.

like car piled high with fire wood, a small tank car as water tender, and three small open passenger cars with curtains rolled up and its seats filled with dignitaries." It traveled at fifteen to twenty miles per hour from Cleveland to Wellington and back. By November, when rails had been extended to Shelby, two trains passed through West View each week.

If that had remained the township's only railroad line, some development likely would have shifted to West View at the expense of Olmsted Falls. But in 1853, the Toledo, Norwalk and Cleveland Railroad (later the Cleveland and Toledo Railroad) laid tracks. They went east–west right through the middle of the township—and Olmsted Falls. Some of the men, including some Polish immigrants, who helped build the tracks remained in Olmsted.

The railroads created local depot and track maintenance jobs. But the blessing was mixed; they also created problems such as getting over tracks before the railroads were required to build crossings. Another problem was that cattle, and sometimes humans, would get hit by trains. In addition, the trains' shrill whistles disturbed the peace.

Village on the Move

The large bridge the railroad built over the west branch of the Rocky River in Olmsted Falls might have been used to move a former seminary from what was then Seminary Road (now Lewis Road) across the river to become the Grand Pacific Hotel. The building moved to its present location no later than 1858. Thomas Brown ran the hotel. The 1939 Olmsted Falls Homecoming program reproduced wording from a ticket to a Thanksgiving party on Thursday, November 25, 1858, at "T. Brown's Hotel." The ticket cost two dollars. Music was provided by Stanton's Harp Band.

By the time the building was moved, Olmsted Falls had been a village for more than a year. Incorporation became official on April 7, 1856. In the first election, just twenty-six residents cast votes. They elected Brown as the first mayor, with H.S. Howe, Newton P. Loomis, William Smith, Thomas Bradwell and George Knight as councilmen. W.S. Carpenter was the first recorder. Village officials conducted business in the same Methodist church basement as the Olmsted Township trustees.

Unfortunately for Brown, a one-year mayor, he did not run the hotel long. Within a few years, he disappeared on a journey to deposit money in a Cleveland bank. Some people assumed he had run off with the money. However, years later, his skeleton was found in a gulch near what is now Columbia Road. The skull had a bullet hole in it, so apparently robbers killed Brown.

Expanding the village did not take long. In 1857, the adjacent hamlet of Plum Creek merged with Olmsted Falls—the first annexation in Olmsted and one of the simplest.

Catholics Arrive

Another sign of growth was the 1856 founding of the first Roman Catholic church: St. Mary's. This was just nine years after the creation of the Diocese of Cleveland for about ten thousand Catholics in northern Ohio.

In 1939, the Reverend Joseph Walsh, pastor of St. Mary's of the Falls, wrote that John Reynolds and his family were the first Catholics in Olmsted Township. They arrived in 1849, when the first railroad was built. Railroad work brought many Catholics to Olmsted. Walsh wrote that an "influx of Irish, German and Polish Catholics insured the life of the church in the village and demanded the formation of a parish."

Olmsted's first Catholic Mass was held in Calvin Geer's barn, although Geer was Protestant. Masses were held in a log schoolhouse from 1851 to 1854 and then at James Hickey's home, where an Elyria-based pastor would visit bimonthly. The diocese sent Father Louis Filiere to organize St. Mary's in 1856. He held Masses in Richard Pollard's house for two years. In 1858, Filiere bought Newton Loomis's 1834 house for use as a parish house

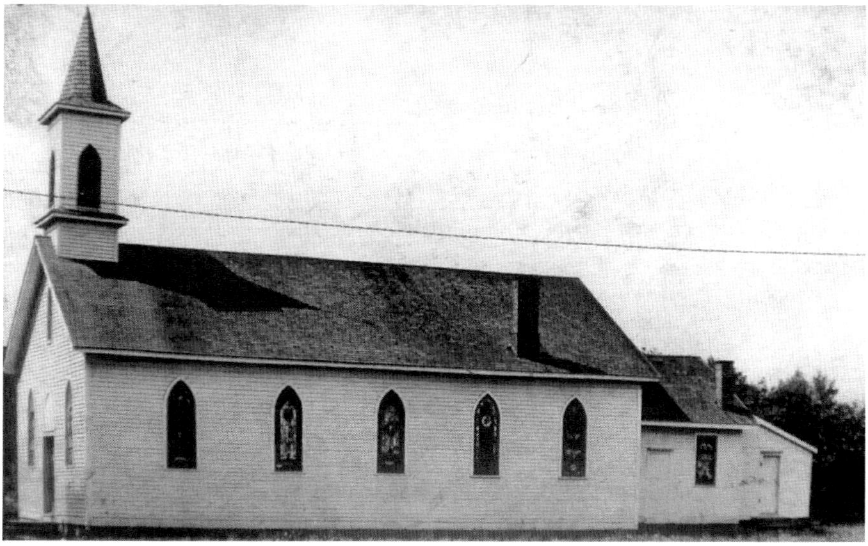

Although it was expanded by the time this photo was taken, this is the St. Mary's church that rolled down the street in 1873.

and briefly as a church. Also in 1858, the parish bought another lot along Columbia Street (now Main Street) and built a small wooden church there.

Holzworth gave the following explanation for why Filiere chose that location on the northern end of downtown Olmsted Falls:

> *In 1858 this was a large knoll that sloped sharply to the river. It was this knoll that appealed to the pastor* [as] *a fitting place for a church and because Father Filiere was born, raised and educated in France; in traditional French taste,* [he] *planted a vineyard from his home and church to the river in the valley.*

St. Mary's remained there only fifteen years. In 1873, Father E.J. Murphy bought several lots totaling four acres at the corner of Columbia and Hamlin (now Bagley Road) Streets. One lot included a stone house, which he repaired and made into a new parsonage. Murphy then had the church building moved on rollers to the lot just south of that parsonage. But moving did not interrupt church business. Even while the building was rolling down the road, an infant, Rose Sanderson, was baptized in it.

GRIT

The reason for St. Mary's move might have been related to another development in Olmsted Falls: the opening of a quarry near Plum Creek. In other words, the pleasant knoll where Filiere had planted his vineyard had acquired a noisy, dusty industrial neighbor. It was no longer a quiet, pastoral location for church business. In 1879, Johnson called the post–Civil War years in Olmsted

> *uneventful, as is the case with most farming communities, after the close of the pioneer era. The most important event has been the opening of quarries of building stone along the banks of Rocky river, of the same quality as the celebrated Berea stone, which is taken out only a few miles distant.*

The quarrying occurred in both Olmsted Falls and West View.

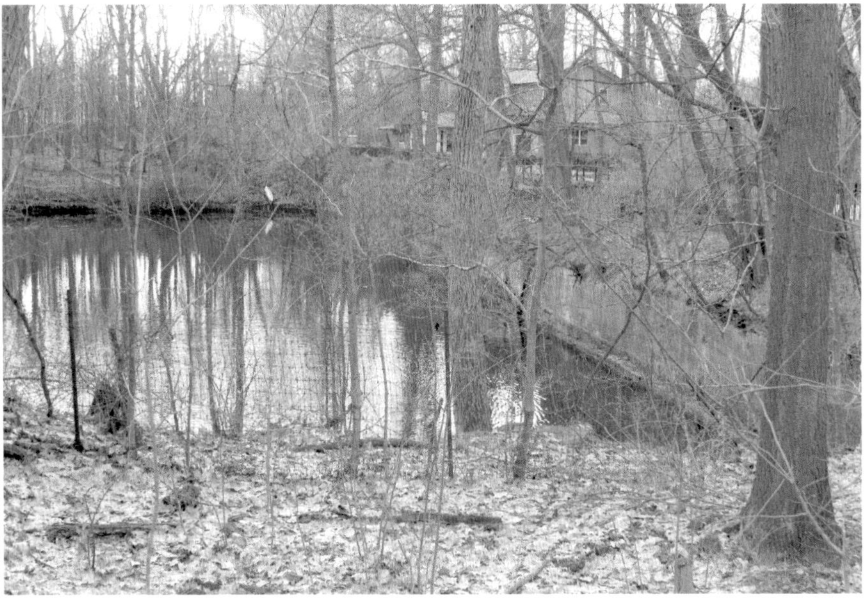

Water fills the huge pits with straight-cut chiseled sides of the former West View quarries, along East River Road just north of Sprague Road. Nearby are blocks of stone that had been carved out of the ground but never hauled away. In a few places, rusted bolts several inches long protrude from large stones, suggesting they once held a greater industrial structure. Grindstones and sandstone blocks left over from quarrying also are found throughout much of David Fortier River Park in Olmsted Falls. *Photo by Jim Wallace.*

Opening the Road

By the 1870s, not all of Olmsted's major roads had been built yet. In particular, residents were eager for a direct road between Olmsted Falls and Berea. Initially, Nobottom Road, which then crossed Rocky River, offered the shortest route between the two communities. In 1864, Gib Doolittle built the first bridge across the river along what is now Water Street. It offered better access to Berea, but Olmsted residents were not satisfied.

"The citizens of Olmsted Falls and Berea must feel interested in having a direct road between the two places," the Olmsted correspondent for the *Advertiser* wrote in June 1870. "Such a road, it seems, was laid out some time ago. How many will take hold of this matter and open up the road?"

In early July, Berea was reported ready to open the road to the town line. The county commissioners had promised to build a bridge across Rocky River once the road was opened. But work had to wait until after the late summer harvest.

The *Advertiser* reported in early September 1870 that road-building work would begin on the nineteenth:

> *Let all who are willing to assist in this be on hand with necessary implements—grading to be done, stumps to be removed, and work common to a new road. Every citizen in the two villages is interested in opening the road, and we hope to see a good force on hand.*

On September 23, the *Advertiser* announced, "We are happy to report that the 'direct road' to Berea has been opened. We trust the county commissioners will take immediate steps to have a bridge built across the branch of Rocky River."

The roadway acquired the name Irish Road because of residents of Irish descent on both ends: a man named Murphy on the Berea end and Olmsted's James Hickey, who had the honor of being the first to drive a team of horses across the roadway. But the bridge did not come soon.

On April 11, 1876, the county commissioners came out to inspect the location for the bridge. A large crowd watched as county officials surveyed and staked the ground on both sides, but they had trouble determining the river's width. Attempts to throw a line attached to a stone from one side to the other were thwarted. Even the strongest arms could reach no farther than midstream. Eventually, they had a dog named Fred swim across the river with the line. Because someone failed to hold onto the line, the dog had to do it a second time. The width of the river was determined to be 138 feet. The headline in the *Advertiser* about the event was: "A Dog Gets a Government Contract."

By the end of August, stonework for the bridge was in place, and work on the iron structure began. But in September, scaffolding holding workers and much ironwork collapsed. Several workers fell, but none was injured seriously.

"The new bridge is completed, and is a substantial structure," the *Advertiser* reported on October 5. "It will compare well with any bridge in the county if not in the State."

Business

In the 1870 census, Olmsted Township's population, not including Olmsted Falls, was 1,152 residents in 259 families with 260 dwellings. Olmsted Falls had 384 residents in 90 families with 70 dwellings.

An 1874 Cuyahoga County atlas listed fourteen Olmsted Falls merchants:

L.L. Fitch, proprietor of Olmsted Falls Hotel
W.W. Mead, manufacturer of harness, saddles, collars, whips, etc., at 39 Main Street
L.B. Adams, dealer in stoves and hardware, and manufacturer of tin, copper and sheet-iron ware, eave-troughing, milk cans and dairy tinware generally
Joseph Bartlett, real estate agent, office over Moley's Store

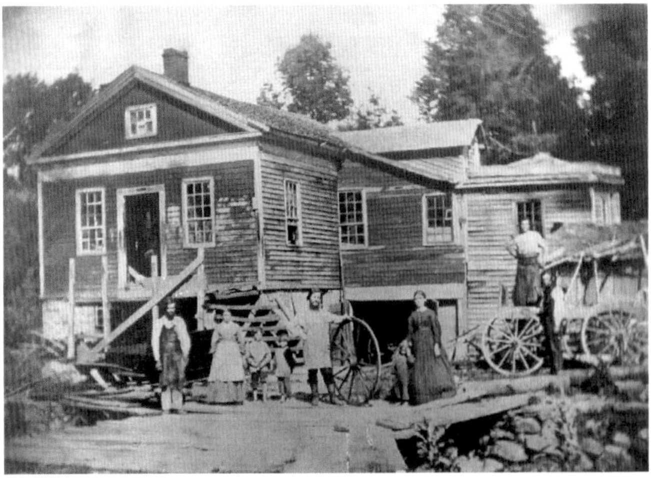

Florin Peltz established a wagon shop in Olmsted Falls (current address 7486 River Road). He died at age fifty-two in 1870. His son, Joseph, established a drugstore and then the hardware that became Peltz & Simmerer's.

A. Osborn, dealer in family groceries
H.O. Fitch, dealer in dry goods, groceries, hardware and notions
H. Moley, merchant tailor and dealer in readymade clothing and gents' furnishing goods, 21 Columbia Street
K. DeRooi, manufacturer and dealer in boots and shoes, 59 Main Street
R. Pallard, dealer in dry goods, groceries, notions, boots, shoes, hats, caps, etc., Main Street
L. Barnum, manufacturer and dealer in block and grindstone, also oak, ash and hickory lumber, bent felloes, etc.
William Suell, dealer in dry goods, groceries, notions, boots, shoes, caps, etc, Lot 31, Olmsted Township
N.P. Loomis, dealer in drugs, medicines and family groceries
Y.A. Rice, proprietor of steam sawmill. Furnishes all kinds of building lumber, on Lot 17, Tract 6
W.S. Carpenter, station agent and justice of the peace

That map listed just one West View merchant: "L.C. Tanney, dealer in groceries, drugs, medicines, perfumery, toilet articles, books and stationery; also proprietor of cheese factory, capacity 400 cows or 20 cheeses per day."

Notably missing from Olmsted Falls merchants, in addition to several saloons owners, was Ed Damp. In 1873, he took over operation of the mid-town gristmill from Colonel H.N. Whitbeck.

Although Loren Fitch was listed as running the hotel, it had a series of proprietors. A March 1872 published notice said Nicholas Moley had acquired the hotel. In January 1873, Fitch took over. In April 1875, W.S. Carpenter took possession and renamed it Hotel DeCarpenter.

Even though Carpenter advertised the hotel as elegant, a newspaper article at the time indicated that many visitors were not so elegant. It said that between October 31, 1874, and April 1, 1875, 425 tramps had stayed there. The township trustees had been providing each tramp a night of lodging and a free meal. When the trustees reversed that policy in March 1878, the *Advertiser* noted that "there is not a tramp within one hundred miles of this place that does not know where the township clerk lives. Just as long as they are fed, just that long will they tramp."

Carpenter left the hotel business less than two years after he started. Frank Dougherty, a former railroad crossing flagman, bought the hotel in May 1877 for $2,000. He made improvements in the hotel and its stables.

In 1873, Olmsted got its first telegraph office on the second floor of Moley's store just south of the railroad tracks on Columbia Street. But it closed in

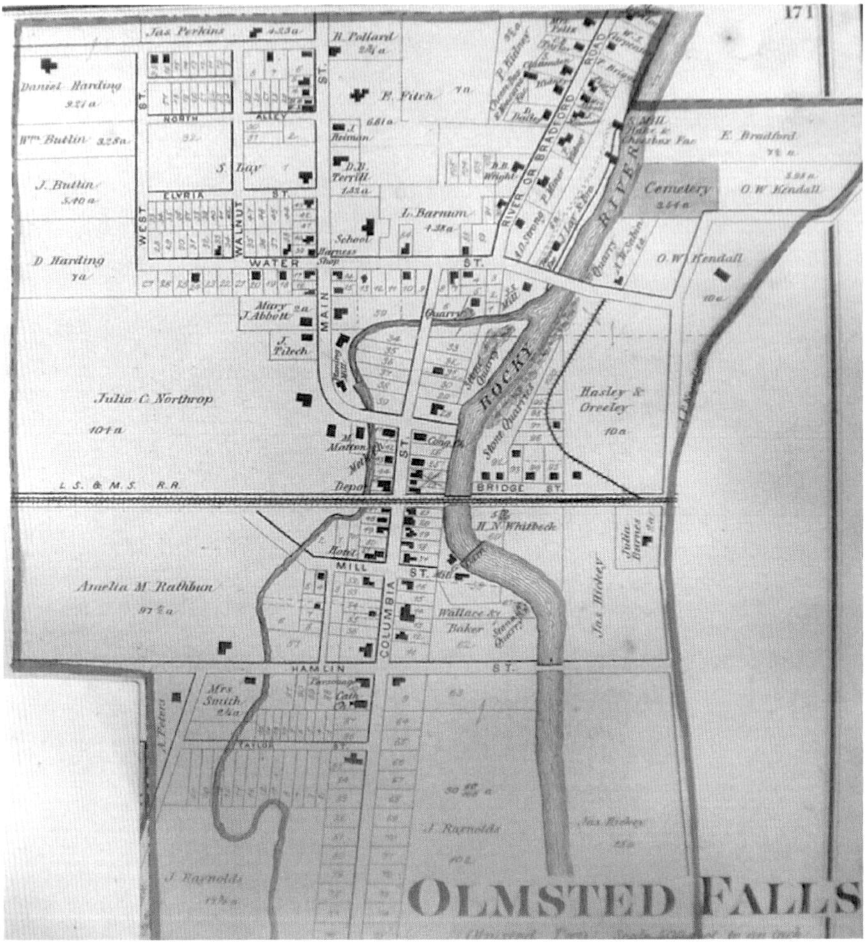

This 1874 map shows the locations of quarries, mills and the school in Olmsted Falls. Some of the street names were different then.

January 1874. In November 1875, another telegraph office opened. It lasted until May 1876. The establishment of a permanent telegraph office awaited another development: construction of a new railroad depot.

DEPOT DELIVERY

Rumors that Olmsted Falls would get a new depot circulated as early as 1872. In January 1875, the *Advertiser* reported:

The people of this village are determined to have a new Depot. The money is nearly all subscribed to purchase the ground to be used for that purpose, and the Railroad Company have agreed to build the Depot and put everything in shape the coming season.

The Lake Shore and Michigan Southern Railway prepared ground for the depot that March, fenced the property in June and began grading the land in August. But by October, some people were impatient. The *Advertiser* reported, "If the new depot does not progress faster than it has for two or three weeks past, it will not be occupied during the lives of the present generation." By March 1876, some people suggested that "the depot is a grand humbug," but in April, the frame was erected. By July, the building was almost complete.

"The new depot is completed at last," the *Advertiser* reported in October 1876.

Mr. Barnum, the station agent, took possession last Monday. Olmsted Falls has a good depot, furnished in good shape with a waiting room for gentlemen and one for ladies, with a dressing room attached. There is also

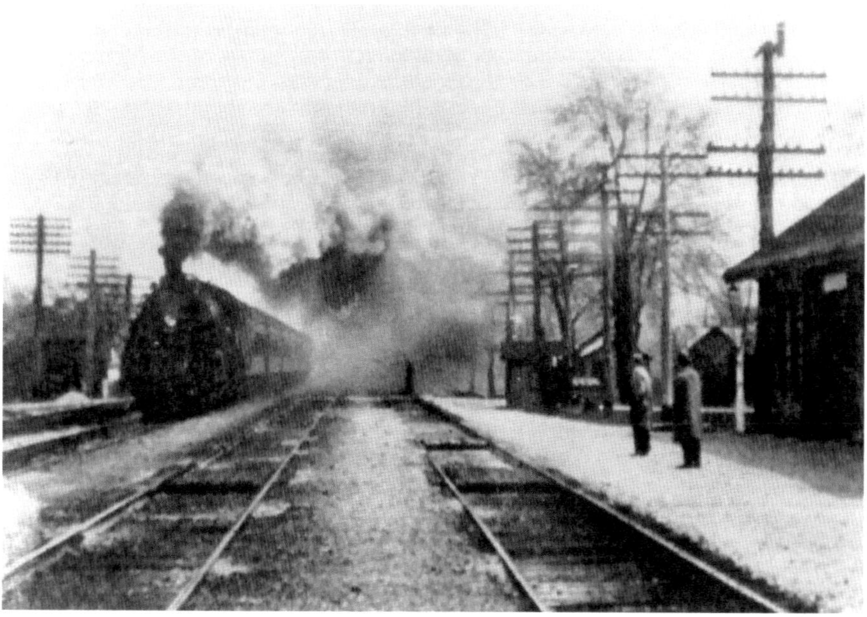

Years after it was built, the Olmsted Falls Depot was moved to the eastern end of South Depot (now Garfield) Street, where it stands today near Brookside Drive.

> *a large freight room, a ticket office and telegraph office, with night and day operator. There is only one disadvantage, it is much to* [sic] *far away to one side of the village.*

The depot was at the western end of South Depot Street (now Garfield Street) near Division Street (now Mapleway Drive). "When we got our new depot, we expected that all our inconveniences, present and future, were removed," the *Advertiser*'s Olmsted correspondent wrote in December 1876.

> *We must say that we are a little disappointed. The management of affairs at the depot is in competent and willing hands and all things about it appear exceedingly well. But it is so far off. It costs our merchants as much to bring their goods from the depot as the shipment from the city.*

Water Power

In 1876, Ed Damp, who had rented Whitbeck's mill, bought it and developed it into a prominent business in Olmsted Falls. In the year following Damp's purchase, the mill ground 13,078 bushels of grain.

In February 1877, the ice-filled Rocky River flooded at West View, destroying the dam at the mill there and a railroad bridge at the Rocky River Stone Co. quarry. But it took only a few weeks to restore the bridge, and by April, work resumed at the quarry. However, another flood in February 1878 destroyed the dam again. No sooner was it replaced in September 1878 than the river rose again and swept it away. The dam was rebuilt that November.

Internment and Interment

After experiencing frequent problems with drunks, transients and burglars, Olmsted Falls built a two-celled jail in the summer of 1878. "This place has furnished its share of criminals this summer, and with one exception they have been punished," the *Advertiser* reported.

Olmsted had two public cemeteries in the 1800s. One was the Butternut Ridge Cemetery, started in 1821. Nearby residents bragged about their beautiful "City of the Dead." The other cemetery was Turkeyfoot, started in 1854 on the outskirts of Olmsted Falls. In the fall of 1878, Turkeyfoot received "long-needed improvements" with new walks and a drive. Township trustees also gave it a new name, Chestnut Grove, although the name Turkeyfoot never faded from use. The next year, the trustees turned their attention to Butternut Ridge by awarding a $1,000 contract for construction of a vault. In 1887, Turkeyfoot got its own vault, which was declared "an excellent piece of workmanship from the skill of a practical builder, Mr. S.C. Broady."

There is a story that persists today that a woman accused of witchcraft was buried at Turkeyfoot. Dan Hill, cemetery superintendent, said in 2007 that he doubted that story because a cemetery is consecrated. "They would not bury an unholy person in a cemetery on consecrated ground," he said. "So there's a very good chance that it could not be a witch. But if you look at the old cemetery drawings, that lot does not appear in the original cemetery drawings, so maybe it's outside the cemetery."

St. Mary's of the Falls created its own cemetery along Irish (Bagley) Road in 1874.

Modest Growth

By the late 1870s, despite the quarries, West View consisted of "a store, two or three shops and about thirty houses," Johnson wrote. But he listed several businesses in Olmsted Falls, including four general stores, two drugstores, one tailor shop, three blacksmiths' shops, three shoe shops, one tin shop, one gristmill, one broom factory, one felloe shop and one lumberyard.

The business elsewhere in Olmsted Township was agriculture, and rural life was tough. An *Advertiser* correspondent from the southwestern part of the township referred to it as being "that unheard of corner of Olmsted." The reporter also referred to cornfields that still needed to be hoed and "the ruined and desolate appearance of many of our homes."

The 1880 census showed that Olmsted Falls had a population of 404, a gain of 18 since 1870. Olmsted Township had 1,415 residents, a gain of 263.

Separate Ways

In 1880, about two hundred Butternut Ridge residents petitioned to divide the township into two voting precincts: one at Butternut Ridge and one at Olmsted Falls. The attempt upset people in and around Olmsted Falls, who circulated their own petition in opposition. The change did not occur, but it sowed seeds of division.

That division was apparent in 1882, when the township trustees wanted to build a town hall. Butternut Ridge people expressed concern that the building would be larger than needed, creating too large a debt. Nevertheless, plans were drawn, and the trustees bought a lot in Olmsted Falls that July, but construction bids came in too high. Aware of the skeptics, the trustees decided that their architect had designed an $8,000 building instead of the $6,000 structure they expected. So they had him rework the plans. In September 1882, they awarded a $5,510 contract to William Trayte of Cleveland for a building seventy-six feet long, forty feet wide and one story high. The main hall was to have a gallery with seating for one hundred people.

An elaborate town hall dedication ceremony on Friday, January 19, 1883, had music, speeches, food and dancing, but not many people from Butternut Ridge. People in Olmsted Falls took that as a slight. But D.K. Huntington of Butternut Ridge said it wasn't. He noted in the newspaper that four of five "old time residents" from Butternut Ridge who were invited to speak at the ceremony did so. However, in his denial of a snub, Huntington confirmed growing antagonism from Butternut Ridge when he asserted "the fact that this part of the township is 'opposed to everything' in which the south part of the township is interested."

Even though the town hall project exacerbated division between Butternut Ridge and the rest of Olmsted, it also illustrated a unity between the township and the village that later would diminish. The township built the hall in the

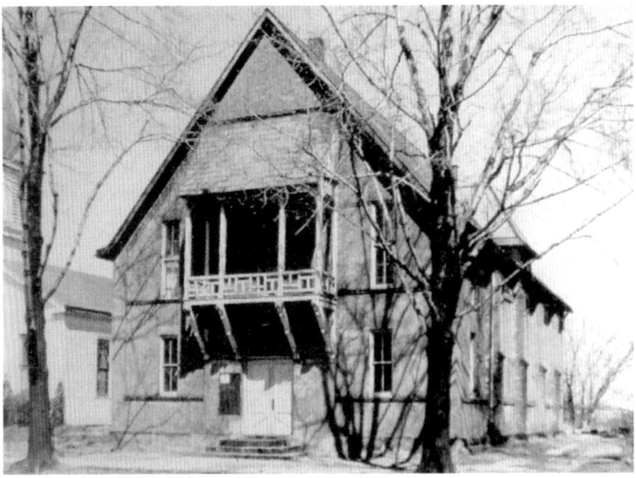

The town hall was the center of township and village activities for several decades.

middle of Olmsted Falls for the township and village governments to share. In many elections before and after that, it was common for individuals to fill township and village offices simultaneously. For example, in 1875, Henry B. Northrop was elected township clerk and an Olmsted Falls councilman. In 1884, W.D. Bennett was elected clerk of both the township and the village, and G.B. Dryden was elected treasurer of both.

But the town hall was not built well. By December 1883, new troughs had to be installed because water was running off the building's front instead of the back as intended. A year later, the trustees had an iron rod installed in the middle of the building "to prevent the walls from continuing on their outward course." They also had to stop a leak near the chimney. In January 1885, that chimney still had problems. When the township clerk started a fire in the fireplace, smoke drove everyone out of the building. One trustee climbed up on the roof and knocked off part of the chimney to clear blockage.

Rushing Waters

Olmsted had bigger problems. On the night of February 2 and throughout February 3, 1883, heavy rain fell after a cold spell had caused thick, heavy ice to form on streams in the area. The Rocky River had one of its biggest floods on record. One writer suggested that the river had never "presented so high an uncontrollable appearance" since the flood in the Bible.

Fearing damage from blocks of ice, residents in the West View area tried to break them up using explosives with limited success. "About 3:30, a fearful sight was presented," the *Advertiser* reported. "Far up the stream above the dam was to be seen what appeared in imagination like a huge iceberg, broken in pieces. On rushed the angry water in all its mad fury—bearing on its tide, its burden of ice, timber and all sorts of floatwood, threatening rain and destruction to everything that came in its way." At least four bridges and the dam at West View were destroyed. Residents feared the mill built by the Hoadleys seven decades earlier would be ruined, but it survived with just minor damage.

Downstream in Olmsted Falls, the flood wiped out the dam at Damp & Difford's mill at an estimated loss of more than $2,000, badly damaged Joseph Lay & Company's broom factory at an estimated loss of $3,000 and destroyed a county bridge over Plum Creek. Lay immediately pledged to rebuild his factory. "We have been here 25 yrs. and this is the highest by at least 5 feet that the river has been up within that time," he told the newspaper. Within weeks, Lay replaced his washed-away boiler, but it took until August for Damp & Difford to resume grinding grain. The company replaced the destroyed dam with one made of Berea sandstone. It was 13 feet high and 175 feet long with a width of 3½ feet at the base and 2 feet at the top.

Repairs took longer at West View, partly because of subsequent floods in late February and late May. When the river was high, people had to take long detours to cross it. It was several months before the bridge along the county line (Sprague Road) was replaced. It took until January 1884 before the former Hoadleys' Mill, then owned by Thomas Chambers, resumed operation. But another winter flood soon carried away part of the dam again. West View area residents chipped in with money and labor to repair it because Chambers was broke from the first repairs.

Hometown Improvements

Telephone service reached Olmsted Falls in 1883. A line connecting Elyria and Cleveland went through the village in June. By November, several residences were connected.

The village council decided in the spring of 1884 that Olmsted Falls needed a bandstand in the public park (Village Green), as well as a five-foot-wide sidewalk on the park's west side. Village businessmen petitioned for the bandstand, which was built by early July for $150. A month later, a chain fence, "which can be used for hitching teams," was erected along the west side of the park.

The streets of Olmsted Falls brightened in the evenings in the mid-1880s with the gradual erection of streetlights. "Still they shine!" a writer in the *Advertiser* proclaimed in January 1886. "Our street lamps are doing fine work and three new ones have been added." Soon, West View boasted its own streetlights.

An important component of community life in and around Olmsted Falls started in 1887 with the formation of Post 634 of the Grand Army of the Republic, a Civil War veterans group. Also that year, Tom Stokes built what was called "one of the most substantial and commodious structures in the town" near his sawmill at the Plum Creek falls. He used the first floor and basement for the storage of fertilizers, lime, cement and other commodities. The second floor became the GAR meeting hall. (The building is now a private residence at 7835 Columbia Road.) The GAR post took charge of Decoration Day ceremonies at the Butternut Ridge and Chestnut Grove Cemeteries. The post and its auxiliary, the Women's Relief Corps, also staged many social events.

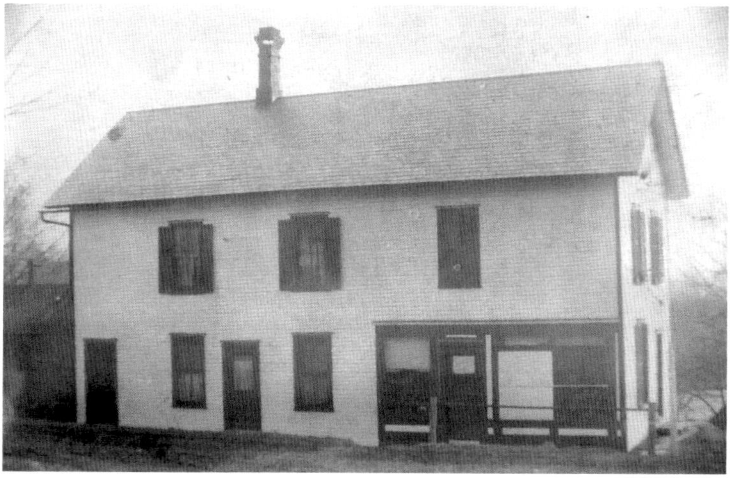

The GAR Hall was both a meeting place for veterans and a storage facility for mill operator Tom Stokes.

Big Stone

The formation of the Cleveland Stone Company by George H. Worthington in 1886 ended the days of quarries operated separately by individual owners. The company acquired quarries in Olmsted Falls, West View, Berea, Columbia, Elyria, Euclid, Kipton, North Amherst, South Amherst and LaGrange. In Olmsted Falls, the company soon built a new stone-sawing mill.

In 1888, Cleveland Stone built a spur track from the main railroad line into its Olmsted Falls quarry by going over Main Street (now Columbia Road) and then through Stokes's lumberyard and across Plum Creek near the falls on a trestle. The track then went along the steep bank on the south side of the creek. The bridge on the northern end of Columbia Street (now Main Street) had to be raised so the quarry track could go under it.

But early enthusiasm for Cleveland Stone waned among Olmsted Falls residents. Construction of the spur track tore up Main Street (now Columbia Road) for months. Six months after the track was completed in May 1888, an Olmsted Falls correspondent complained:

> *It has been two years now since the sidewalk was taken up and the road made nearly impassable to accommodate the Cleveland Stone Co., which has and is no doubt doing much for our town. But is it necessary thus to make one of the most used thoroughfares impassable that they may take their time to do the work in.*

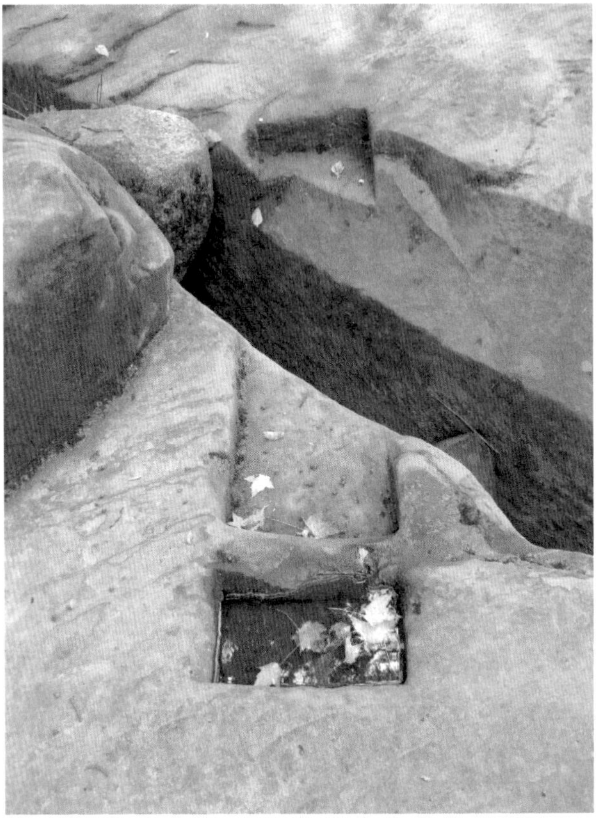

Left: The stone creek bed at the Plum Creek falls still has rectangular holes where posts for the railroad spur trestle once were anchored. *Photo by Jim Wallace.*

Below: The current park path under the covered bridge is where Cleveland Stone's railroad spur ran. *Photo by Jim Wallace.*

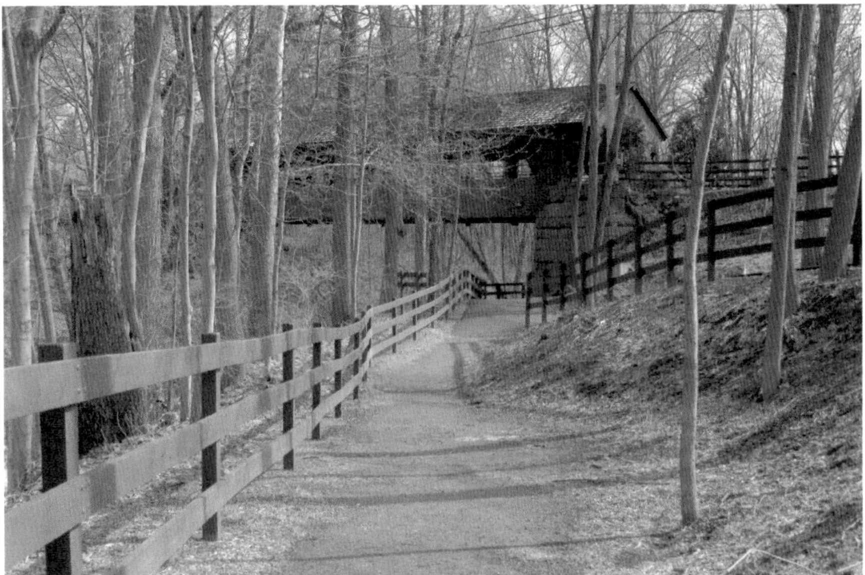

The village council argued about the problem in December 1888, but the relationship with the company did not improve soon.

"The people of the Falls begin now to realize that a corporation is truly a heartless and a soulless body," the *Advertiser* correspondent wrote in January 1889.

> *The belief has been unified by the operations of the stone company in stripping preparatory to spring quarrying. In crossing the sidewalk with their loaded wagons at various places they leave great deposits of clay upon the walk making it a thing next to impossible to pass. Columbia street* [now Main Street] *is all tore up and the pedestrians drag off untold quantities of soil.*

It is not clear when or if Cleveland Stone ever repaired the streets.

Hardware and Wheels

Through the years, many businesses came and went, changed partners and changed locations in Olmsted Falls. A significant change occurred in August 1892, when J.P. Peltz & Co. bought the old hotel. Joseph Peltz had operated a drugstore in the early 1880s. In 1882, he added hardware to his stock. In 1884, he installed a soda fountain. Peltz welcomed his brother-in-law, Philip Simmerer, into the business. After they acquired the hotel, they remodeled it, and in February 1893, they moved their stock into it.

Beginning late in 1894 and throughout 1895, Butternut Ridge residents were excited about the construction of a streetcar line by what was then the Cleveland & Elyria Electric Railroad. The line had a big effect on the lives—and attitudes—of residents. Eleven months before any of them would ride on it, it was suggested that residents were becoming more metropolitan. Some might have recalled the criticism in 1882 from an Olmsted Falls resident who dismissed Butternut Ridge's brass band and sidewalks and wrote that "if North Olmsted ever expects to keep pace with the Falls' enterprise, they must erect a couple electric masts and a viaduct, and then wake up to find they are just a street railroad behind." Well, after the rail line opened in mid-December 1895, Butternut Ridge had less reason than ever to feel connected to the rest of the township. The interurban line provided travel to downtown Cleveland in just about forty-five minutes.

"The electric road is a big institution in spite of the rather enormous fares that are charged," the *Advertiser*'s Butternut Ridge correspondent wrote late

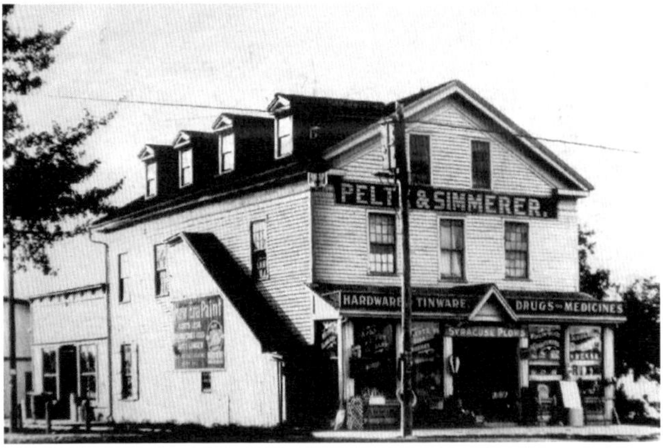

The establishment of Peltz & Simmerer Hardware in the former hotel was the beginning of one of the town's longest-lasting businesses—seventy-eight years in one location.

in 1895. Soon, newspaper routes and mail delivery began using streetcars. By November 1897, an Olmsted Falls writer expressed regret that

> *there is no immediate prospect of securing an electric railroad. Nearly every other village in the neighborhood of Cleveland now has an electric railway. But we have the Lake Shore road, which accommodates our people with regular morning and evening trains.*

Meanwhile, other wheels were moving. First, in 1893, it was reported that "roller skating mania has broken out" in Olmsted Falls. By 1897, bicycles were the rage with riders at Butternut Ridge, West View and especially Olmsted Falls, where forty new bicycles were reported that May: "Wheels! Wheels! In the head, in the feet, in the talk, in everything past, present and future."

In August 1899, a Butternut Ridge reporter wrote:

> *The novel sight of a horseless carriage was seen by some of the residents of this neighborhood a few days ago. The vehicle came over the hills and through Cedar Valley then back toward the city. It was said to go eighteen miles an hour and make as much noise as a steam engine.*

Another invention also began entertaining Olmsted residents: the phonograph. In January 1896, when one youth group in Olmsted Falls held an evening of phonographic entertainment, it was reported, "Nothing of this kind has ever been given here, and it will be a rare opportunity for everybody to sit and listen to a phonograph for an hour or more."

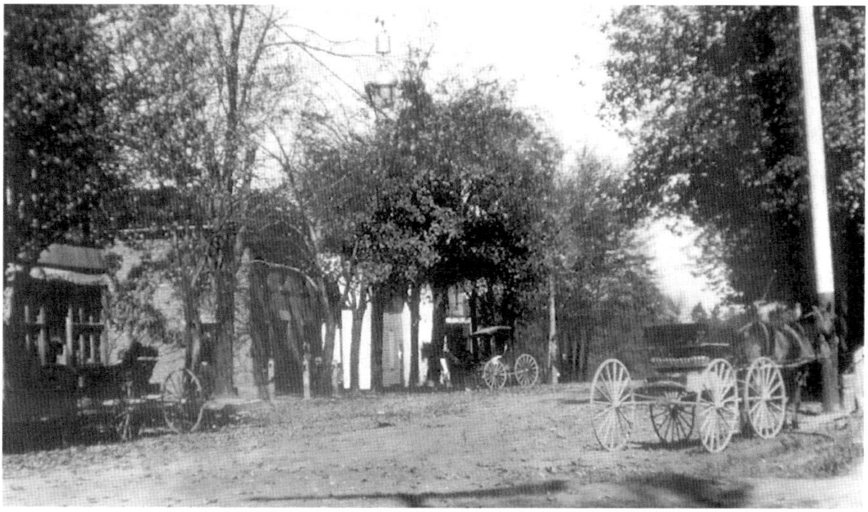

Olmsted streets in the 1800s were dirt—or mud.

On the Edge of Change

Olmsted Falls had a population of 380 in the 1900 census, a modest increase from 342 in 1890. Among the businesses in Olmsted Falls were Peltz & Simmerer's hardware/drugstore, Damp's Mill, Arthur Dodd's grocery store, a farming implements business owned by Henry Fenderbosch and James Burns, a blacksmith shop and a few saloons. At least two women, Francis Dodd and Eva Stokes, had millinery shops. West View had a smaller business district with a few stores. Butternut Ridge was growing with new and expanding businesses and residences thanks in part to the streetcar line.

At the falls along Plum Creek, Tom Stokes operated his water-powered sawmill and cider mill. Several others cut lumber in township woods with portable, steam engine–powered sawmills. Ed Kidney's bending works was running day and night turning out steam-bent, wooden carriage parts. Olmsted Falls had less quarrying than in the past. More stone was quarried in West View.

Many roads and streets had been built and improved in the latter half of the nineteenth century. Bridges had been built—and sometimes rebuilt. Some hills were leveled to make the roads smoother. Ditches were dug to improve drainage. Sidewalks were laid in Olmsted Falls, West View and Butternut Ridge with slate or sandstone from the quarries. But in those days, when horse and carriage had not yet yielded to horseless carriage, the roadways were dirt, which became mud in late winter and spring to the dismay of residents.

Much would change soon.

MODERN TIMES

1901–1944

The dawn of the twentieth century brought many changes beyond numbers on the calendar, both gains and losses, including a community divorce.

The urge for separation began outside of Olmsted but soon spread within. Directly north of Olmsted Township, Dover Township extended all the way to Lake Erie. That changed in 1901, when northern residents voted 126 to 33 to break away and form a new municipality. Initially, the new municipality was called Bay Hamlet, but it was later renamed Bay Village.

Similarly, northern Olmsted Township around Butternut Ridge had been growing apart from Olmsted Falls and the rest of the township for decades. The 1890s establishment of the streetcar line, giving the area better access to Cleveland and Elyria, only exacerbated that tendency. Residents oriented east and west, rather than south, for commerce and other affairs. Early in the 1900s, residents followed the lead of Bay Hamlet. Ten square miles of northern Olmsted Township united with four square miles of southern Dover Township. On December 8, 1908, North Olmsted held its first municipal election. It began the year 1909 as a village.

Meanwhile, important changes occurred in Olmsted's economic base. The opening of a quarry at Columbia Station in 1901 benefited West View, where it was reported, "Houses for rent are in good demand here." But that same year, Olmsted Falls lost its most productive citizen. Ed Kidney's Cleveland Bending Works had a voracious need for wood to make wagon and carriage parts. Kidney often traveled in the South, "prospecting for timber land." In 1901, Kidney and his family moved to Memphis, Tennessee, where he took charge of the New Bending Works. His former partner, Gus Leutkemeyer, then moved equipment from the Olmsted Falls factory to one in Metropolis, Illinois. Some Olmsted residents followed him. Although Kidney returned to Olmsted Falls in 1904, the village never regained his former industrial output.

In 1904, Olmsted almost got another railroad. The Pittsburgh and Lake Erie Railroad bought the right of way through the village and the township. But the project was abandoned when it proved difficult to cross swampland near Lake Abram in Berea. (Two piers meant to hold the railroad bridge across the Rocky River still stand. They can be seen south of the bridge along Bagley Road.)

Hooking Up

It was also a time for modernization. Although some Olmsted residences and businesses had received telephone service as early as 1883, Bell Telephone and Citizens Telephone rapidly put up more lines in the early 1900s. When one line from Olmsted Falls through West View to Columbia Township went up in 1901, an *Advertiser* reporter remarked that "there are some here who are soon going to have the privilege of conversing from their residences over the wire with Berea friends."

About a dozen years later, electric service came to Olmsted. The George E. Milligan Co., which operated a power plant in Elyria, erected a line along Dutch (Bagley), Usher and West Roads. Olmsted Falls was so eager for electricity that poles were erected in the spring of 1913, well before the company was ready to provide the lines. The village set up a transformer plant at the corner of Dutch and Usher Roads.

A couple of years later, another utility reached Olmsted. The *Berea Enterprise* correspondent reported it with self-mocking humor in June 1915:

> *The new gas mains are nearly all laid, and it is expected that we will soon have the gas turned on, many residents already having their houses piped, and keeping the plumbers busy. Hurrah—now all we need to be in the metropolitan class is waterworks and sewers, street cars, apartment houses, fire department, police and a municipal popcorn stand.*

Whether or not they had popcorn, Olmsted residents did have movies. By 1914, motion pictures were shown every Saturday night at the town hall.

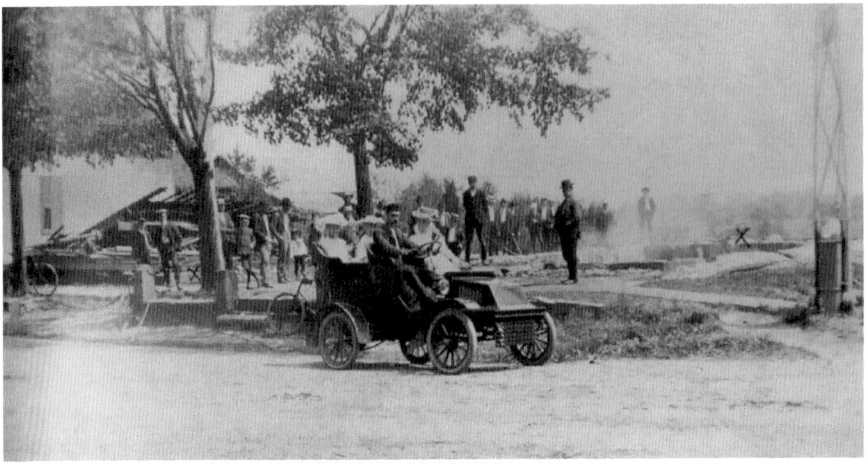

The automobile became a preferred means for many Olmsted residents to see the sights, such as the scene of the fire that destroyed the first Odd Fellows Hall in August 1903.

Automobile use increased steadily. So did road improvements. Some main roads were paved with bricks. The county commissioners had Irish Road (later Bagley Road) paved from Berea to Olmsted Falls in 1909 at a cost of $60,000. It was fifteen feet wide with stone curbs. About a year later, Columbia Street from the center of Olmsted Falls to the county line at West View was paved. Concrete and asphalt eventually took the place of bricks.

Newspaper reports of auto accidents replaced reports of accidents involving horses. In January 1913, the *Enterprise* reported that "a number of village motorists" from Olmsted Falls attended the Cleveland automobile show's opening. "It is reported a number of 1913 models will be seen on our streets this spring," the paper said.

Automobiles also brought new problems. In 1913, the *Enterprise* noted, "Many local auto enthusiasts can't see the numerous 15-mile signs in the village—their eyes should be opened." In 1915, the paper complained that the village was not enforcing an "ordinance compelling vehicles to carry lights after dark."

FIRE AND FLOOD

No matter how modern Olmsted was becoming, the old nemeses of fire and water caused much damage early in 1913. A January 8 fire destroyed W.G. Locke's store, where it started, as well as Joe Anton's tin shop and a two-story

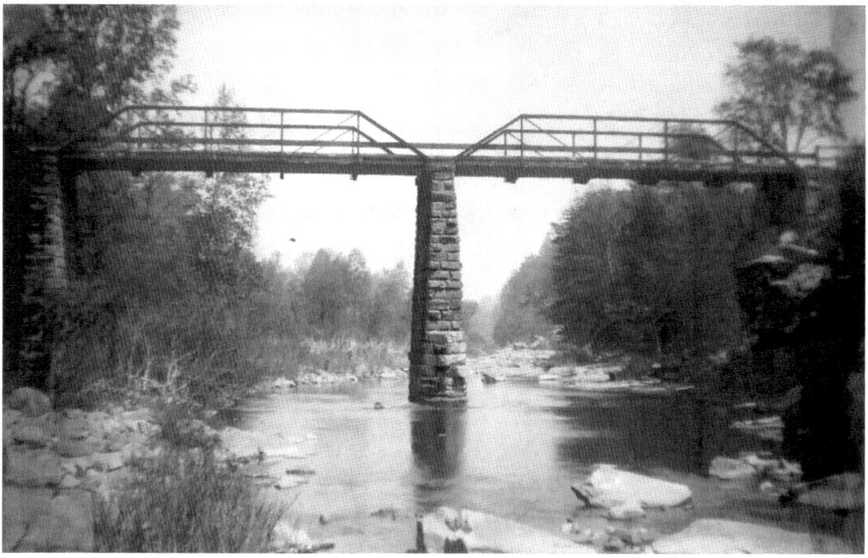

Tall stone columns supported the Water Street Bridge before the 1913 flood destroyed them.

house. Fortunately, the fire department saved Joe Peltz's house. In the 1920s, the Depositors Bank Building took the place of the burned-out buildings.

On March 25, 1913, the Rocky River flooded as it had in February 1883. The river destroyed bridges, including one on the county line at West View and the 1864 Water Street Bridge in Olmsted Falls. The Water Street Bridge had plank flooring supported by three stone columns, one on each side of the river and one in the middle. As Charles Bonsey, born in 1893, recalled in 1982:

> *Something heavy, maybe a tree or a log or something, hit that* [middle] *abutment, knocked it down, and down went the bridge. And incidentally, a schoolmate of mine—a girl that was in my class in school—was driving a horse and buggy across the bridge, coming from east to west, and she just got across and the bridge went down.*

The flood wrecked Damp's Mill in Olmsted Falls and washed away what was left of smaller mills along the river. Bonsey recalled the destruction of the Damp's Mill dam:

> *Everything was floating down—big trees and everything like that—and eventually it must have knocked a couple of stones loose. When it got one*

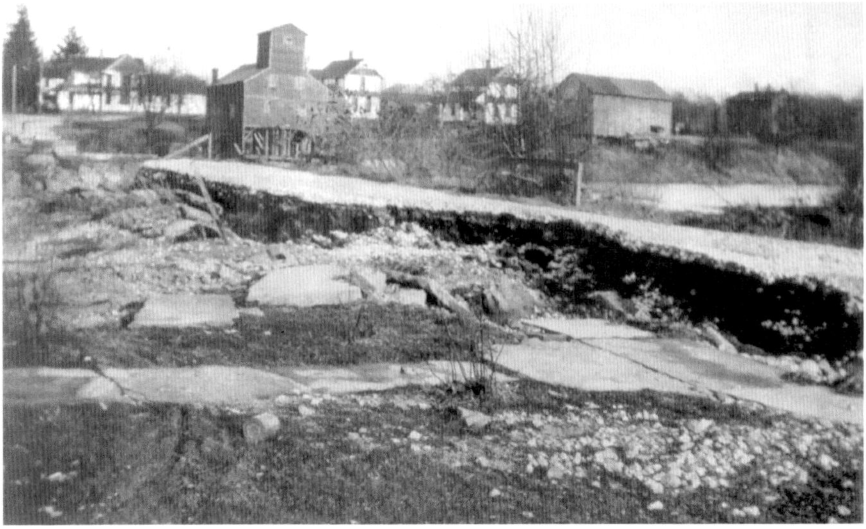

The mill owned by Thomas Chambers at West View remained standing even though water went all around and through the building. The 1913 flood also destroyed the bridge and much of Sprague Road.

> *or two stones, it weakened the rest of them, and down went the dam...Of course, it put the mill out of business, because there was no more water power. It washed the whole dam out.*

GETTING TOGETHER

A spirit of consolidation seemed to arise in Olmsted in 1915. In January, the Methodist Episcopal and Congregational churches, across from each other on Columbia Street, began considering a merger. Over the years, they often had shared Sunday school classes and some services.

"A great deal of thought and hard work is being put on the Community Church proposition," the *Enterprise* reported that February. "It is a good thing. Help it along."

By late 1916, each church had appointed a committee to work out details of unification. In January 1917, the two churches adopted articles of federation, creating the Olmsted Community Church. The former Methodist church was used for worship services, while the former Congregational church was used for Sunday school.

The movement to consolidate township and village schools also began early in 1915 but moved a bit faster. On March 8, 1915, an all-day public meeting featured a Cleveland professor as the main speaker. "Come with your lunch and boost the meeting," the *Enterprise* wrote. One month later, the newspaper reported, "Rapid strides are being made toward the centralizing of schools." Later that April, village residents voted fifty to thirty-two to form a single school system with the township. By June, they were one. In 1916, the consolidated district opened a new centralized school and became the county's first district to eliminate all one-room schools.

New Developments

The Roaring Twenties began with an uproar in Olmsted Falls over a proposal for a tannery at the former bending works site along River Street. About three hundred people at a town hall meeting in 1920 objected to it. The village council passed an anti-nuisance ordinance to keep the tannery out. Something more lasting also resulted: a set of zoning codes.

In 1927, a few hundred people in the southeastern corner of Olmsted Township chose to incorporate as the Village of West View. It encompassed 1,250 acres—1.95 square miles. By the 1930 census, the village had 345 residents. In 1928, the village approved a $10,000 bond issue to prepare a suitable town hall. The old West View schoolhouse, remodeled for that purpose, opened in August 1929.

During the 1920s, many real estate developers pushed out from Cleveland to establish suburban housing subdivisions. Improved transportation from automobiles, bus lines and commuter trains made it easier for people to work

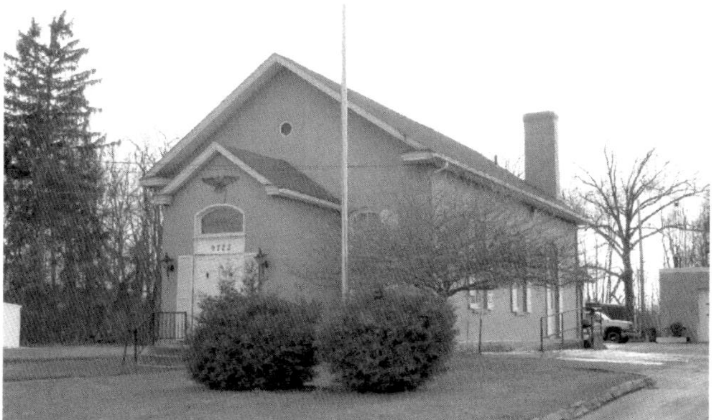

A former school became West View's town hall in 1929. After the 1971 West View–Olmsted Falls merger, the new community had two town halls, this one called South Hall. *Photo by Jim Wallace.*

in the city while living in the suburbs. In the *Cleveland Plain Dealer* in April 1926, Arthur M. Goldsmith of Falls Realty, Inc., singled out Olmsted Falls as ripe for development because the New York Central Railroad ran right through the community. Other reasons he cited were scenic beauty along the Rocky River and the acquisition by the Metropolitan Park system of the nearby Cedar Point area, as well as "good air and an ever increasing number of good roads and improvements of all kinds rapidly going in."

About that time, the Olmsted Falls Development Co. advertised 60- by 150-foot housing sites in the Caine-Garfield Allotment, a subdivision "in the heart of Olmsted Falls, right in the path of the new Metropolitan Boulevard." The ads mentioned a commuting time to Cleveland of only twenty-five minutes via the New York Central.

But Olmsted residents were wary about too much development. For example, in 1928, Olmsted Falls Council adopted a zoning ordinance that confined businesses to just three blocks. The village also decided that any future industrial plants would be relegated to a large tract on the northwestern edge of town. That year, Olmsted Falls was called "the smallest town with a Kiwanis Club."

However, people behind a proposed subdivision in the township had big plans. In the spring of 1929, a full-page newspaper ad for Homelinks proclaimed, "Play all day in your own back yard." It showed spacious homes with fronts facing wide avenues and backyards abutting the golf course. "Step through the garden gate, your garden gate, and you're on the golf course," the ad said. "Eighteen of the sportiest holes in the state—that's Homelinks as it will look in a few years. Homelinks, the man-made Paradise." Further, the ad showed photos of available transportation, including service from trains, streetcars and the Olmsted Falls Bus Co., as well as good roads.

The developer, L.H. Heister Jr., Inc., had created subdivisions in Lakewood and elsewhere. Homelinks was to be bordered on the north by Butternut Ridge Road, on the east by Columbia Road and on the south by John Road. It would have been half in North Olmsted and half in Olmsted Township. "Now is the time—Right Now!" the ad said. But the time wasn't right.

Five months after that ad, the stock market crashed. The Great Depression began. The Homelinks that emerged was a more modest eighteen-hole golf course without a surrounding housing development. Its clubhouse was on John Road, not Butternut Ridge, using John Hall's former homestead and barn. In 1944, some of the original project's land was divided into lots with one-hundred-foot frontage along Columbia and John Roads and put up for sale.

Another portion of the originally proposed Homelinks development became Springvale Country Club, owned by the Biddulph family mostly on land that John Biddulph had bought in 1860. The clubhouse was Springvale Ballroom, which had been built in 1923, along Canterbury Road in North Olmsted. It began as a nine-hole course in 1936 but expanded to eighteen holes stretching almost to John Road, just east of Homelinks, in 1953. At that time, the *Plain Dealer* called the combination of Homelinks, Springvale and the North Olmsted golf course (north of Homelinks and west of Springvale) "the largest concentration of golf activity in northern Ohio." (Later, the City of North Olmsted acquired Springvale.)

Another victim of the Depression was a proposed modernization of Olmsted roads. Several roads would have been extended, including: Cook Road east to River Road, Fitch Road south to Usher Road, Schady Road east to Columbia Road and then on to Metropolitan Boulevard, Metropolitan south to West View and under the railroad tracks, Water Street west to Division Street (Mapleway Drive) and Cranage Road west to Fitch Road. Most ambitious would have been rerouting Columbia Road so that, as it headed south, it would not have turned to go through the Olmsted Falls business district but would have gone straight through a tunnel under the railroad track to meet up with Orchard Street and then would have continued south behind St. Mary's. Finally, it would have curved southeastward below Taylor Street to connect with the existing Columbia Road. In addition, most of the roads would have been expanded to a width of eighty feet.

A Change of Pace

The 1930s were not a time for ambitious projects. One notable exception was the Works Progress Administration (WPA) project in Olmsted Falls. It converted the former site of quarries and mills where Plum Creeks flows into Rocky River into a municipal park. The WPA was the largest of the New Deal agencies during the Depression. It employed millions of otherwise jobless persons in public works projects.

Another connection Olmsted Falls had with the Roosevelt administration was Raymond Moley. As a young man, he had served as school superintendent and mayor of Olmsted Falls, but the village couldn't hold him. He was a professor at Columbia University in New York when Franklin Roosevelt sought his help during the 1932 presidential campaign. Moley assembled Roosevelt's "Brain Trust," a group of advisors mainly from Columbia. He wrote speeches for Roosevelt before and after the election. But Moley later grew disillusioned with Roosevelt. In 1933, he became an editor at *Today*

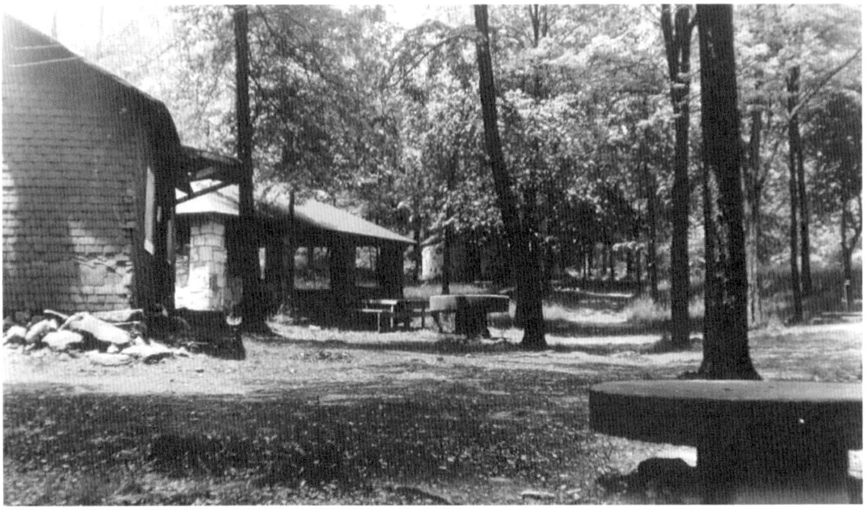

The WPA workers took old grindstones and stone blocks left over from quarries to make steps, tables, shelters and a bridge in the Olmsted Falls park.

magazine, which merged in 1937 with *Newsweek*. He stayed there for another thirty years. He also wrote newspaper columns and nineteen books.

On July 19, 1938, Olmsted Township held an election using a single voting booth at the corner of Nobottom and Columbia Roads to consider whether the township should incorporate as the Village of Olmsted. The issue failed, but that election marked the first of a long series of efforts to either incorporate the township or annex all or parts of it to neighboring municipalities.

After several years of the Depression, Olmsted residents were ready for a big celebration in 1939. They had held homecomings each year since 1922 with games and other activities at the Village Park (Village Green). But the 1939 celebration was bigger, partly because it marked 125 years since Olmsted's first settlement. The homecoming was a three-day affair, beginning August 11, at both the district school and the park. Activities included free movies, concessions, a baseball game pitting "Coffee-Pot Dodgers" (married men) against "Olmsted Falls Cubs" (single men), a rodeo, modern dancing, old-time dancing, a community Sunday dinner, a commemorative program featuring an address by Cleveland Mayor Harold Burton and a roll call of former students with the ringing of the old Union School bell. The final day's activities attracted a reported seven hundred people.

The homecoming's seventy-two-page souvenir program is like a printed time capsule of Olmsted life. Articles tell of the history of the village, township and community organizations. The program has more than twenty photos of Olmsted and its people. An aerial shot reveals more farmland than houses around the school. Most buildings were clustered along the Columbia Road corridor. A few photos show buildings that would be gone soon, including the Union Schoolhouse, the former Congregational church and the old St. Mary's of the Falls.

Among Olmsted advertisers in the program were: United Farmers' Exchange, Charles Barnum's United Food Store, Ritter's Farm, Henry N. Walkden Insurance, Smith Brothers (general contractors), Schultz's Barbershop, Rudy's Barbershop and Beauty Salon, Hecker-Hickey-Eick (plasterers), Maynard's, P. Simmerer & Sons Hardware, Agnes O. Schritz (postmaster), Falls Repair Shop, Olmsted Falls Lumber Company, Olmsted Falls Shoe Repair, Olmsted Game Club, Homelinks Golf Club, Naber's Service Station, Olmsted Cleaners, Heib's Dinner House, Schritz Motor Sales, James H. Burns Real Estate, Radio Electric Shop, Fenderbosch's Edward's Food Store, Parker's Service Station, Olmsted Beauty Shop, E.R. Graf Service Station and R.F. Hecker's Sohio Service Station.

Town Halls Come and Go

The program showed one building with a drawing rather than a photo. That was because the Olmsted Township Hall was still under construction at the corner of Fitch and Cook Roads. "When completed, this building will be the center of township activity, in that it will provide a central location in which to hold Trustee meetings and elections, and will adequately house township records," Sam Jaeger wrote. The facility might have been adequate, but it never has been spacious. A quarter century later, historian Walter Holzworth commented, "The building was pleasing in design but far too small for any other purpose than to accomodate [*sic*] the chairs and tables for the trustees and a few seats for spectators."

Another building pictured in the homecoming program was the old town hall in Olmsted Falls. It was torn down in 1940 to be replaced by a building made from local sandstone. This was another WPA project, but the WPA had trouble getting enough skilled laborers. "It was my headache to see that that building was completed," Charles Bonsey, who was mayor in 1940, said years later. "Well, the government hadn't put out enough money to build. The walls were up with no roof on, and WPA pulled out." So Bonsey complained to the WPA and got work resumed. Its open house celebration

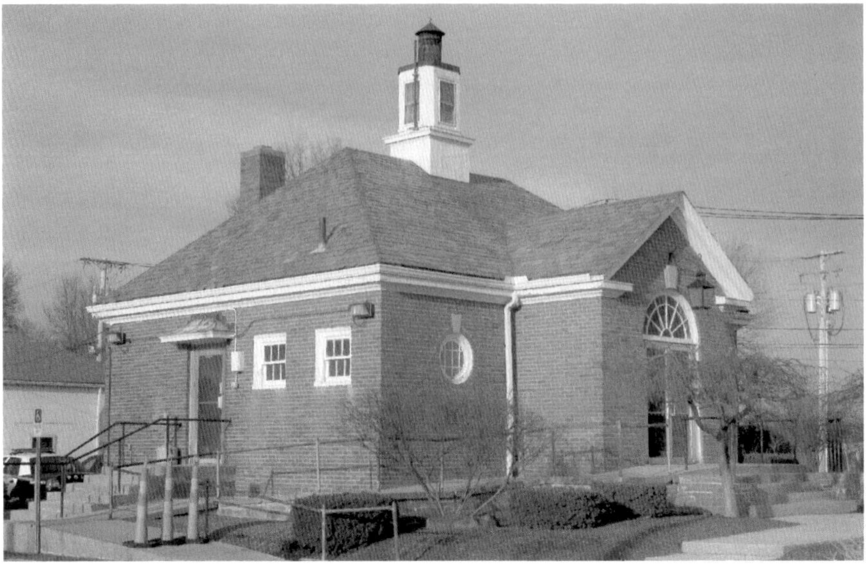

Olmsted Township Hall's construction heralded a break from years when village and township officials shared space in one government building in Olmsted Falls. *Photo by Jim Wallace.*

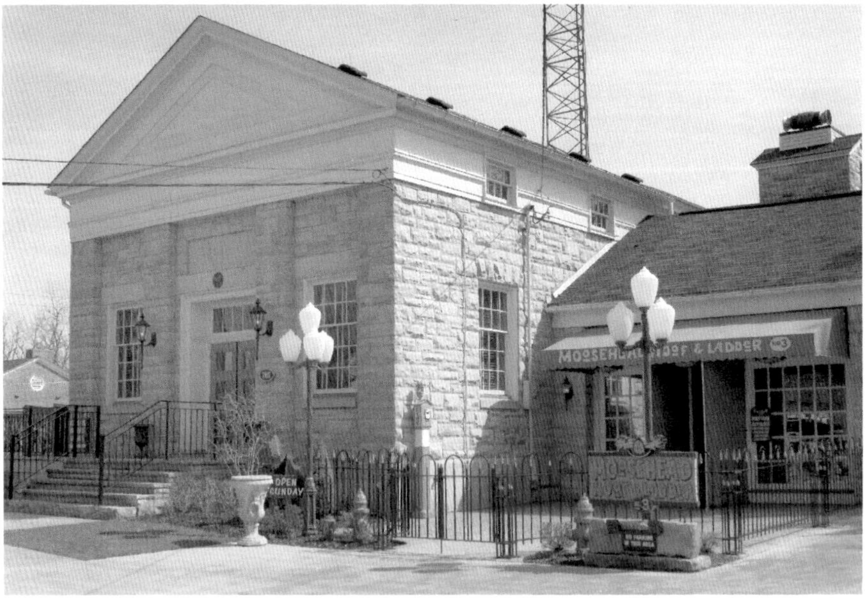

After the 1971 Olmsted Falls–West View merger, this building was called North Hall. In 1983, it was renamed the Bonsey Building in honor of the mayor who made sure it was completed. *Photo by Jim Wallace.*

was on April 13, 1942. It was expected to cost $18,000, but it ended up costing $30,000. The building included space for the council chamber, the police department, the fire department and a jail.

Contented Living

An April 19, 1941 *Cleveland Press* article described Olmsted Falls as "content to be nothing more than a haven of restful living, free of the harassments that accompany urban activity." Author Eugene Segal said the community had maintained "a constant vigil to preserve its character."

At that time, Olmsted Falls had only about nine hundred residents and nineteen businesses, including a bank, two groceries, a dry goods shop, an automobile dealer, a delicatessen, an appliance store, two gas stations, two barbershops, a feed store, two automobile repair shops, a drugstore with a soda fountain, a lumber company, a hardware store, a physician's office and a dentist's office. West View and Olmsted Township had several other businesses, but not many.

By the time the town hall opened, the United States was in World War II. Changes would come after the war.

SUBURBAN GROWING PAINS

1945–1989

World War II was barely over before Olmsted Township residents had a new domestic fight on their hands. In November 1945, the City of Cleveland wanted to buy seven hundred acres in the township to build a $4 million workhouse to replace the city's Warrensville Workhouse. The township's large sections of undeveloped land and no zoning restrictions were attractive to Cleveland. But the idea of living near Cleveland's criminals was not attractive to township residents. They also worried that it would devalue their property and cost the school district thousands of dollars it could not afford to lose.

At the time, a township couldn't impose zoning regulations. So residents seized on incorporating the township as a village or annexing it to Olmsted Falls. Two groups circulated petitions for an incorporation vote. One wanted the name Olmsted Village; the other preferred Olmsted Heights, even though the township was one of the flattest places in Cuyahoga County and was no higher than surrounding communities. The trustees accepted the Olmsted Village petition. With 2,250 residents, the proposed municipality would have been bigger than either Olmsted Falls or West View. But at the January 29, 1946 election, township voters rejected incorporation, 217 to 143.

A 12-man committee quickly circulated a petition for annexation to Olmsted Falls. A preelection postcard poll showed 174 township voters preferred annexation, 147 preferred incorporation and 44 preferred no change. But it seemed the petition needed signatures of more than half the township's adult landowners, and no list of landowners existed.

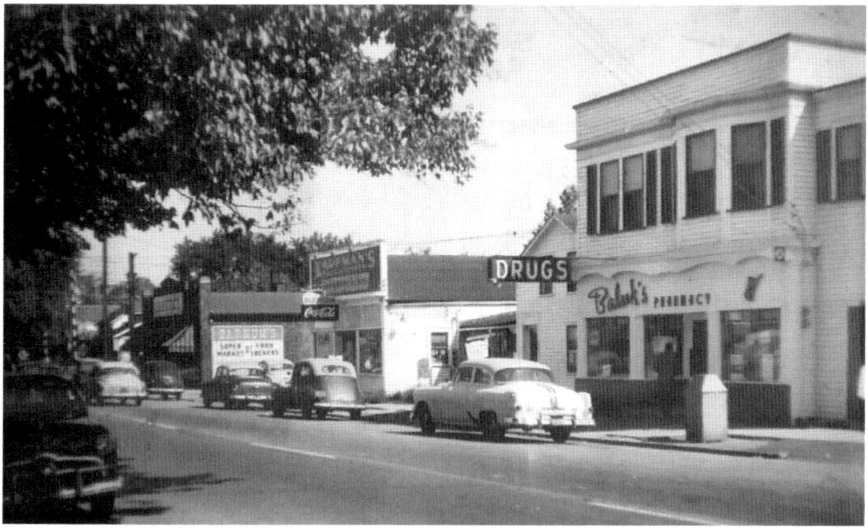

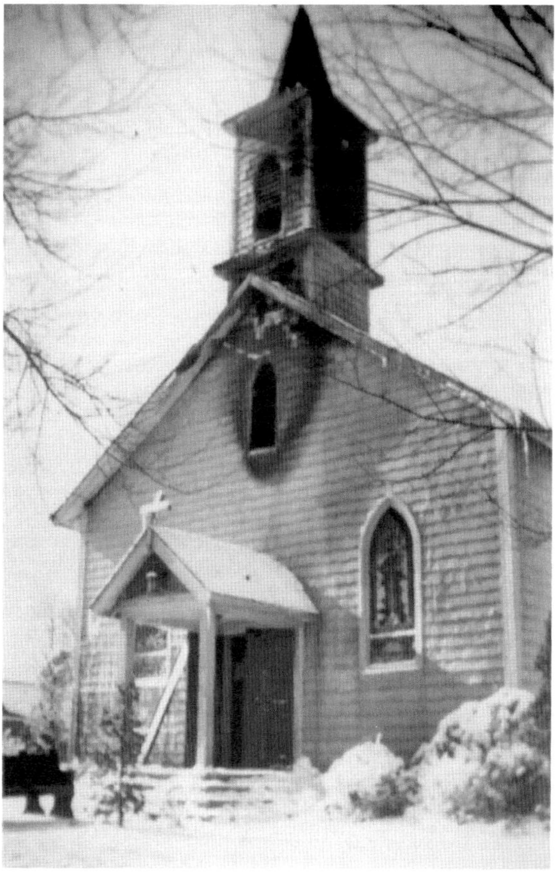

Above: Many buildings in Olmsted Falls' business district survived in the postwar years, but not these shops on Columbia Road. All were gone within a few decades after this early 1950s photo.

Right: The wooden frame building of St. Mary's of the Falls stood at the southern end of downtown Olmsted Falls for almost seventy-five years since it was rolled down the street in 1873. On January 24, 1948, a fire destroyed it. A new building replaced it in 1950.

Meanwhile, the newly formed Anti-Tax Committee of Olmsted Township, led by Township Trustee William Kroessen, circulated petitions against annexation. The township property tax rate was $2.06 per $100.00 of valuation, while the village's was $2.99. Some suggested annexation could result in a $3.15 rate, mainly because the village would take over road maintenance from the county. Annexation opponents claimed that could drive farmers out.

When Cleveland opted for improving Warrensville Workhouse facilities instead of building a new Olmsted Township workhouse, urgency for annexation vanished. By August 1946, annexation supporters had withdrawn their petition.

In 1947, the township-village border changed with the annexation of sixty acres east of Columbia Road between John and Nobottom Roads and five acres along Lewis Road. Also that year, Governor Thomas Herbert signed a bill permitting township zoning, eliminating one reason for annexation or incorporation.

TRAILER TROUBLES

The township was still working on its first set of zoning codes in July 1948 when a new land-use dispute broke out. Gerald Brookins wanted to build a trailer park on fifty-two acres of vacant farmland west of Columbia Road, south of John Road and north of Cook Road. He claimed it would be "a modern trailer park which would be an asset to any neighborhood and a contribution to orderly, healthful and efficient living." But the township and the village united in opposition. On July 12, the village council and the township trustees held a joint meeting attended by about 150 people. They feared new residents in the township, which already had two trailer parks, would strain the school system.

Township officials hurriedly prepared their zoning ordinance, although they were too late to use it against Brookins. Voters rejected the ordinance in November 1948. Zoning opponent William Barnard of Usher Road complained in a letter to voters: "Someone is using police state tactics in a township, where freedom abounds." Township voters approved a zoning ordinance 407 to 160 in July 1952. By then, construction was already underway on the trailer park, which was eventually named Columbia Park.

Hard feelings stirred by the trailer park fight lingered for years. When two of the three township trustee positions were up for election in 1957, it played out as a battle between "trailerites" and "permanent residents." Some township residents were concerned about having "trailerites" as two of the three trustees. If about seven hundred of the expected eighteen hundred voters lived in trailers, they wouldn't have had an outright majority but could have swayed the election. In the end, that didn't happen.

New Construction

The mid-1950s brought construction of the Ohio Turnpike through the township south of Bagley Road and right through the middle of West View. County engineer Albert Porter negotiated with turnpike officials in 1953 for improved alignment in the relocation of Schady and Fair Roads. In 1954, he refused to permit opening the Usher Road Bridge over the turnpike until a guardrail was installed.

In Olmsted Falls, the Olmsted Community Church decided to build one big church instead of continuing to use the old Methodist and Congregational churches. The church began fundraising early in 1954 for a new building just north of the Congregational building.

First, the 1834 Newton Loomis house had to be moved. The church had moved it once before from 8017 Columbia Road, just north of the railroad tracks, to the Main Street site. The house, donated to the village, was moved across the street to become the public library. Until then, the library had been on the top floor of village hall. The new library opened in June 1955.

The Community Church razed the former Congregational church to make room for a parking lot, but it sold the former Methodist church.

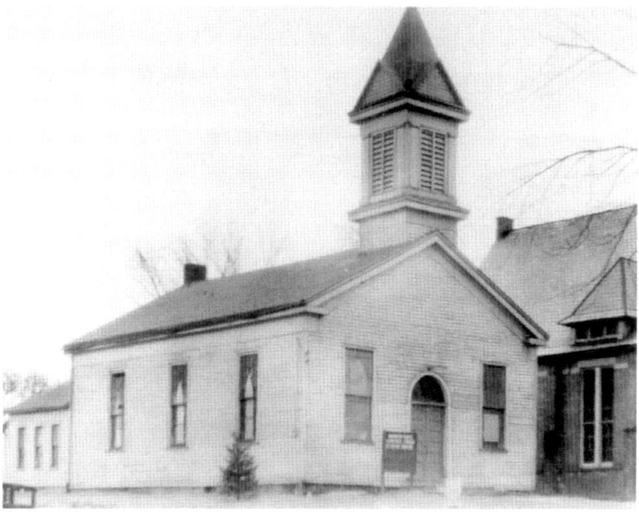

The former Congregational church, seen here next to the 1883 town hall, lasted a little more than a century after it was built in 1848.

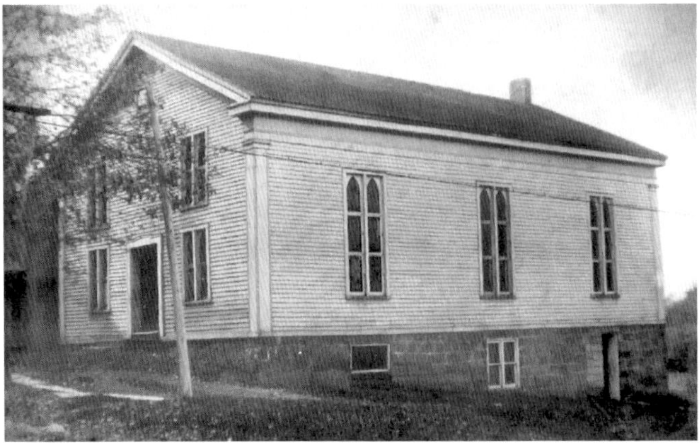

The Masonic Lodge bought the former Methodist church, built in 1853, for $25,000 in 1956. It became Grand Pacific Wedding Chapel after Clint Williams bought it in 2001. He put a new steeple on it. The first one blew off in a 1910 storm.

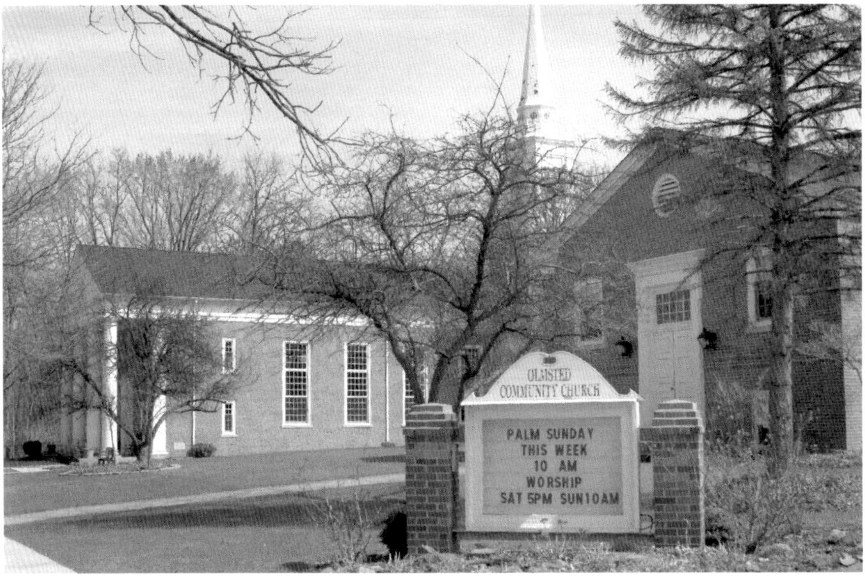

Olmsted Community Church is a prominent structure in Olmsted Falls. Its location is the original site of St. Mary's of the Falls. *Photo by Jim Wallace.*

In February 1956, the church's Fellowship Hall and education wing were dedicated. The cost was $240,000. On April 12, 1959, Philip Simmerer, then ninety-three and still running his hardware store, had the honor of turning the first dirt for a $205,000 sanctuary. He had been a church member since 1889. The congregation of about nine hundred dedicated the sanctuary on March 20, 1960.

Annexation Resumption

New movements to change the status of all or part of Olmsted Township cropped up in the mid-1950s. Late in 1954, North Olmsted considered annexing a portion of the township. North Olmsted wanted land for industrial expansion. It offered water and other services, as well as a lower tax rate, as long as the annexed section also switched school districts.

That effort didn't go very far, but in 1958, the Olmsted Business Men's Association backed another attempt to incorporate the township. It was spurred partly by plans by K&L Builders of Middleburg Heights to build a new subdivision with 232 houses just west of Fitch Road. The new streets would be Elizabeth, Eastwood, Adele and Crestwood Lanes. The big concern was strain on the school district, which already had the county's fourth-highest tax rate.

Trustees wanted to attract industry to the western end of the township, but doing so wasn't easy. Legal advisor Fred Frey said no suburban community could survive on residential taxes alone. He argued that state laws governing townships were inadequate for a community the size of Olmsted and warned that the "worst thing that could happen would be to allow the township to be consumed piece by piece by surrounding municipalities."

Soon, such a prospect arose. Berea wanted to annex a portion of township land. Then, residents around Lewis, Barrett and Nobottom Roads circulated petitions for annexation to Olmsted Falls.

Township trustee Ben Warner joined the effort to incorporate the township as the Village of Olmsted Heights. Some businessmen backing that effort wanted the new village to then negotiate on equal footing with Olmsted Falls and West View for a three-way merger. Trustee William Gilligan opposed incorporation, fearing the township might have to become a city after incorporation if the 1960 census showed it had more than 5,000 residents. He considered the township unprepared for that. In November 1958, township voters rejected incorporation 924 to 552.

Subdivisions Grow

From 1959 through the mid-1960s, developers announced plans for more subdivisions that could have added a few hundred to a few thousand houses to the township. School board members viewed them with dismay. The school system already had built two elementary schools and was struggling financially.

While Olmsted Township fought internal battles over growth, neighboring communities, particularly Berea and North Olmsted, were growing with new subdivisions and retail centers. In North Olmsted, construction of the Great Northern shopping center began in the mid-1950s and kept going for years. It provided Olmsted Falls, West View and township residents with a convenient place to shop but none of the tax benefits.

ZONING WOES

Late in 1960, Fitch Road resident Ernest Miller discovered that Columbia Park had prepared sewer lines, light poles, roads and cement pads for at least 25 more trailers. Township officials said Brookins had not told them about his plans. They thought the zoning code the township had adopted in 1952 had frozen the number of trailers at fewer than 150 in Columbia Park and another 100 combined in the trailer parks on Bagley and Cook Roads. Soon, Miller formed the Home Owners' Committee of Olmsted Township, which entertained a proposal for annexation to North Olmsted of seven square miles of township north of the turnpike and west of the Rocky River. Berea and Brook Park officials expressed interest in annexing the eastern portion. But a few hundred township residents at a January 1961 meeting were cool on annexation, fearing higher taxes.

In February 1961, some residents discovered that Sunset Memorial Park, the cemetery on Columbia Road at the North Olmsted border, was building a mortuary. More than one thousand citizens signed a petition seeking better zoning enforcement. In March, trustee William Gilligan inspected Sunset Memorial. He found not only the almost-completed mortuary but also a new flower shop already in operation and an almost-finished mausoleum. Neighbors were concerned about lower property values. However, the county prosecutor's office told the township that nothing could be done against Sunset Memorial.

On the trailer park, the prosecutor's office maintained that permits issued before township zoning took effect limited the trailer park to no more than 300 units, about twice as many as were already there. However, Prosecutor John Corrigan soon revealed that the Cuyahoga County Board of Health had issued Brookins a permit for 820 units. He also said that zoning restrictions could not apply to Columbia Park because it was in place before zoning. In December 1961, a judge rejected the township's attempt to prevent further expansion at Columbia Park. By then, it had 165 trailers and was preparing for 46 more.

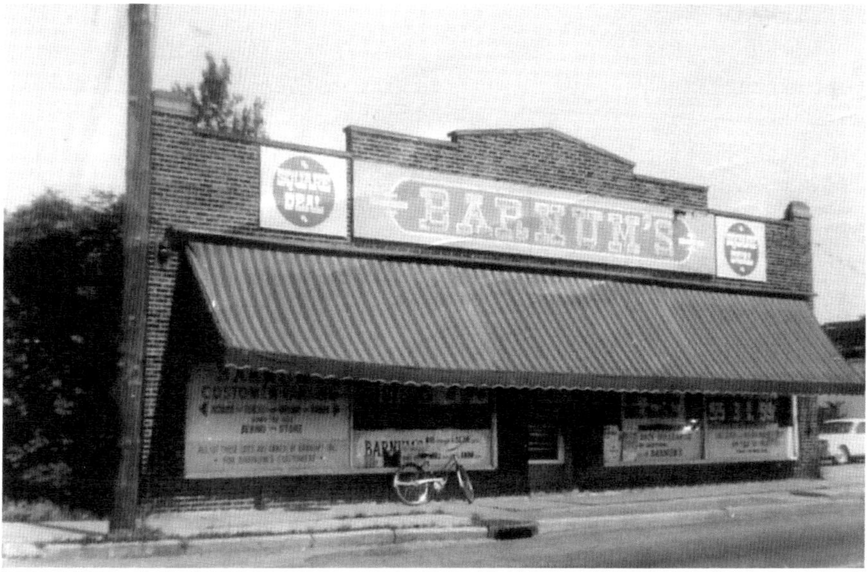

Descendents of early Olmsted settlers operated Barnum's grocery on Columbia Road until it burned down in 1967.

Late in 1961, the township's zoning inspector, Nicholas Bakker, cited Brookins for laying down railroad tracks and having several trolley cars at Columbia Park. Brookins collected old trolley cars. This was the beginning of Trolleyville, USA. The township zoning board reached an agreement with Brookins by March 19 to let the trolleys stay. Within a few years, Trolleyville became a tourist attraction listed by the American Automobile Association and other travel organizations. By 1966, it had sixteen trolleys—including a couple from as far away as Mexico—and a museum at the shopping center. For fifty cents on weekend and holiday afternoons, an adult could ride a trolley from the shopping center to the rear of the trailer park near Fitch Road and back. A child could ride for twenty-five cents. In 1969, Brookins acquired a former Baltimore & Ohio depot from Middleburg Heights and moved it to Trolleyville.

Annexation Influx

A flurry of annexation efforts began in the late 1960s, initially from a new direction. After many efforts over the years from Olmsted Falls, North

Olmsted, Berea and even Brook Park, West View made a bid in early 1968 to acquire the township. That caused Olmsted Falls to revive its dormant annexation effort. Despite the competition, both West View and Olmsted Falls expressed interest in eventual consolidation of the two villages and the township. However, the village that annexed the township first would be in a stronger bargaining position. Township trustees were more favorable to West View's bid.

Other communities were not idle. North Olmsted suggested all three of them should join with it in what could have been a municipality slightly bigger than the original township. Meanwhile, Berea sought annexation of the portion of the township east of the Rocky River. West View mayor Alan Mills expressed concern that if Olmsted Falls would annex the township, Berea might push for annexation of the eastern half of his village, resulting in Olmsted Falls getting the western half.

In May 1968, township voters rejected annexation to Olmsted Falls by a two-to-one ratio. Berea soon released a planning study for the eastern portion of the township. It called for using 380 acres for residences and 526 acres for light industry. The population of the area would have expanded from 535 to about 4,400.

Mayor Mills argued that the November 1968 election could be the last chance to prevent the township from being picked off in pieces. Ohio law required a five-year wait before failed annexation issues could be tried again. Thus, Mills said, it was likely North Olmsted and Berea would be able to get portions of the township before Olmsted Falls or West View could try anew. But township voters again rejected annexation, this time more narrowly: 946 to 1,051. They also defeated a two-mill operating levy, and the township fell into financial trouble. Before the end of 1968, the township clerk, police chief and most of the police force had resigned, and rubbish collections were cut back.

RENEWED EFFORTS

Early in 1969, several annexation movements broke out, including one to annex all the township to West View (using a different section of law than in 1968), three to annex portions to Berea, one to annex Olmsted Falls to West View and another to annex part of the township to North Olmsted. There was even a petition drive for township residents who had signed the petition for annexation to West View to nullify those signatures. A *Plain Dealer* reporter wrote in April 1969, "Somewhere in Cleveland there is a balding, white-haired map-maker who bursts into tears every time he sees another annexation petition from Olmsted Township, Olmsted Falls or Westview [*sic*] Village."

In July, the county commissioners rejected all of the proposals. They said they didn't want a new West View to surround Olmsted Falls. They also rejected creation of "fingers" of Berea sticking into the township. But Commissioner Hugh Corrigan suggested they would give "serious consideration" to annexing the township east of the Rocky River to Berea and the rest of it to a merged Olmsted Falls and West View.

The proposed Olmsted Falls–West View merger got moving. By early 1970, a six-member committee—three members from each village—had worked out an agreement. Although it was commonly called a merger, legally it called for Olmsted Falls to be annexed to West View, but the combined community would be called Olmsted Falls. Existing zoning codes and liquor laws (Olmsted Falls dry, West View wet) would initially stay in place.

The hope was that after the two villages consolidated, the township would join them. Polls indicated that most township residents preferred to form one entity out of the three. Olmsted Falls had about 2,400 people in 1.52 square miles, West View had about 2,500 people in 1.95 square miles and the township had about 7,000 residents in 10.42 square miles. On May 5, 1970, the voters of both villages accepted the merger. The new larger Olmsted Falls came into being at the beginning of 1971. But the effort to join the township to it fizzled.

In May 1972, Mayor Mills asked the state for city status and got it. As Olmsted Falls became Ohio's 231st city, it had about fifty-six hundred residents. Mills said that city status removed much "bureaucratic red tape," such as having to get state permits just to put up a traffic signal, and prevented other cities from trying to annex a portion of Olmsted Falls. It also allowed the school district, in 1975, to become a city school district instead of just a local school district, a move that gave the school board more autonomy.

Air Battle and Border War

By the mid-1970s, southwestern Cuyahoga County communities had quit battling one another over township land and banded together to fight expansion of Cleveland Hopkins Airport. Their main concern was noise, but historic preservationists also raised the possibility that the loud jets passing low overhead could cause structural damage to historical buildings in Olmsted Falls. Such efforts continued through the next few decades.

New housing developments in Olmsted Falls and the township stirred several battles over zoning and other matters and even a border skirmish between the Falls and the township. In 1974, Olmsted Falls erected a barricade of concrete-filled steel drums on Brentwood Drive at the city limit. The city wanted to prevent construction vehicles working on the Brentwood subdivision in the township from using the city's portion of Brentwood Drive, running between Usher and Bagley Roads. The concern was that heavy vehicles could damage the pavement.

On June 7, 1975, township residents, supervised by township trustees, struck back. Using a bulldozer, they removed the barrels. Township officials argued the barrier was illegal and unsafe. However, city residents restored it the next day. A city ordinance provided that the barrier would be removed by January 15, 1980, or after 90 percent completion of the subdivision. In August 1978, councilman David Fortier reported that 193 of the 215 planned houses were finished, so the council voted to remove the barricade.

A BRIDGE TOO MUCH

Another intergovernmental dispute involving Olmsted Falls cost the job of a longtime county official. In October 1973, Cuyahoga County engineer Albert Porter closed the two-lane bridge that carried Bagley Road over Plum Creek. It was a concrete arch bridge in use since 1910. Porter contended that it was ready to fall down. He wanted to replace it with a four-lane bridge, although the outer two lanes would not be used unless Bagley Road was widened. The city wanted only a two-lane bridge.

On May 17, 1975, the city defied the county by removing steel poles and reopening one lane of the bridge to eastbound traffic. That lasted almost one year, until Porter closed it again—and put an eight-foot fence around it—with a court order in his favor.

But Porter quickly fell out of favor with more than just Olmsted residents because of a letter he wrote. His letter responded to one from twelve-year-old Beth Ann Louis, a township resident. She urged him not to widen the bridge because it might scare away wildlife and "because we want our town to stay small." In his letter, Porter criticized her spelling, punctuation, sentence structure and "paragraphing," as well as her reluctance to see Olmsted

Falls grow. He wrote that Olmsted had few cultural amenities, which meant residents had to go elsewhere for sports, arts, shopping and other activities.

"In other words, you are moochers, scroungers, chiselers, and parasites," Porter wrote. The ensuing outrage was covered on newspaper front pages and local television news shows and then carried by wire services nationwide.

Porter, who was seventy-one, had been county engineer since 1946 and a Democratic Party stalwart. But he lost his November 1976 reelection bid in a landslide to Ronald Stackhouse, a forty-three-year-old civil engineer from Cleveland Heights. Although Porter had other problems, such as an investigation into questionable campaign fundraising, many observers credited his defeat to his nasty letter.

New Engineer, Same Problem

Stackhouse soon promised to reopen the bridge to pedestrians and determine if it could handle one-way vehicular traffic again. But within a few months, he decided that Bagley Road needed to be widened through Berea, Olmsted Falls and Olmsted Township, including a four-lane bridge over Plum Creek. By mid-1977, Olmsted Falls Council had quit holding out for a two-lane bridge. The county agreed to build a temporary two-lane bypass so traffic could get through while a permanent bridge was built.

The old bridge came down in November 1977. The construction of the $125,000 temporary bridge began the following February. The barriers came down, and it opened in late July 1978.

Then, nothing happened for four years. By August 1982, a new county engineer, Thomas Neff, proposed replacing the temporary bridge with a $1.1 million permanent bridge, perhaps as soon as late 1983. Again, Olmsted Falls balked—and eventually won. In September 1987, the county opened a new $233,000 two-lane bridge.

By then, two highway changes had occurred just outside the township in North Olmsted. In December 1980, twelve miles of Interstate 480 opened from the Lorain County line to West 139th Street in Cleveland. It had two interchanges serving Olmsted Falls and Olmsted Township: one for Ohio Route 252 near Great Northern and one for Stearns Road. In the mid-1980s, the state relocated part of Route 252 so it split from Columbia Road north of North Olmsted's border with the township.

UNUSUAL REQUEST

In 1976, Brookins wanted to expand again. He had bought about two hundred acres south of Columbia Park extending almost to Cook Road for another five hundred trailers. Unable to get permission from the township, Brookins talked to Olmsted Falls officials about annexation. Zoning regulations had previously kept trailers out of Olmsted Falls, but the city had recently added a mobile home section to its zoning code. Unlike their predecessors who had fought the trailer park, township trustees didn't want to lose it. Trustee Robert Venefra was quoted in the *News Sun* as saying, "They are good neighbors and they provide a tax revenue. If we lose Brookins, we lose Cook Road." He said the township might have to give Brookins what he wanted or risk losing territory and tax revenue. In the end, Columbia Park stayed within the township and continued to expand.

Another township zoning dispute resulted in lasting changes to both the township and the city. In 1978, township voters rejected rezoning for the LaBelle Harbour development that would have allowed the Flair Corporation to build 444 townhouse units on 70 acres and another issue that would have allowed construction of 180 apartment units on 15 acres. In 1981, Flair sought to have 180 acres east of Usher Road and north of Sprague Road, including LaBelle Harbour, annexed to Olmsted Falls. The county commissioners rejected that move, but an appeals court overturned the commissioners' decision in 1983. Then, in October 1984, city council voted down the proposed annexation. In 1987, township voters rejected another rezoning referendum. In 1988, both the county and the city approved the annexation of 206 acres. The border changed.

MYSTERY DEVELOPMENT

A development proposal in Olmsted Falls raised many people's hopes—and then kept them hanging. In January 1975, DEM Investments announced plans for a two-level, Williamsburg-style shopping center with a grocery, bank and several shops. It was slated for the northeastern corner of Columbia and Bagley Roads. But DEM had trouble getting a grocery chain interested. In September 1978, the word was that construction would begin by the following spring. By August 1979, it still was on hold.

In December 1981, Mayor William Mahoney revealed that he had been in secret discussions with someone over developing even more of that corner:

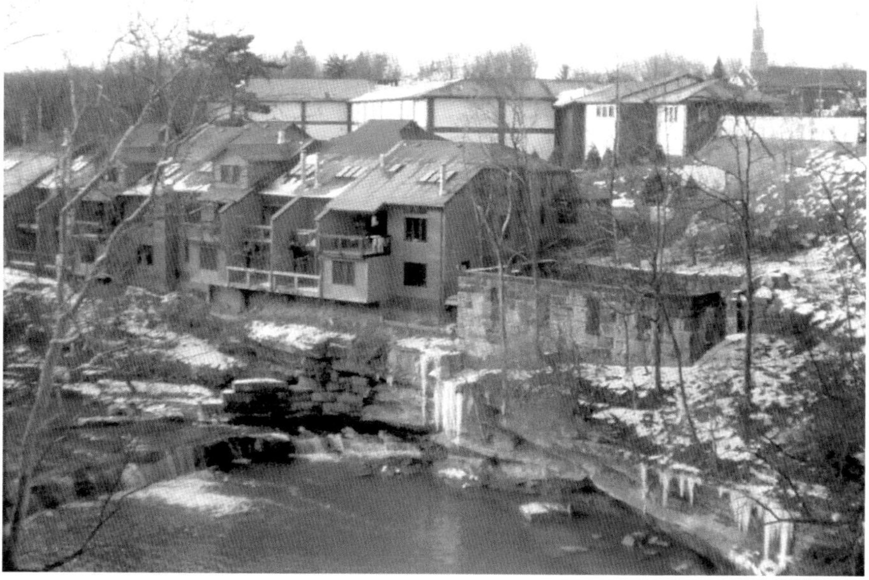

Condominiums were built in the 1980s overlooking the Rocky River behind Mill River Plaza and next to the foundation of Damp's Mill. *Photo by Bruce Banks.*

9.2 acres extending as far north as the railroad tracks. In January 1982, the developer, Rex Associates of Olmsted Township, presented plans for a three-story office building, a bank, several shops, a recreation center, a year-round swimming pool and trails for walking and biking. Also included was a restaurant overlooking the river to be built partially on the foundation of the former Damp's Mill. The development was to be called "The Recentre."

The proposal had strong support from the public and the school system, which wanted additional property tax revenue. But by July, the developer had scaled down the plans, partly because it was unable to buy all the property needed. Plans changed a few more times. The recreation center was dropped. In August 1986, work began on Mill River Plaza with a Discount Drug Mart and other shops facing Columbia Road and condominiums overlooking the river.

Almost Out with the Old

As plans shifted for the northeastern corner of Columbia and Bagley, the opposite side of Columbia Road almost changed. In 1980, National City Bank announced plans to build a red brick "Western Reserve–style" building at the corner of Columbia Road and Mill Street. But that was the location of what was then Kucklick's Village Square Shoppe Annex, the once and future Grand Pacific Hotel. City officials wanted the bank branch but didn't want to lose one of the town's oldest buildings. National City offered to donate the building to the city, but it would have to be moved west on Mill Street and turned ninety degrees to face the street. The bank eventually built its branch on the east side of Columbia Road.

Two years later, in November 1982, Phillips Planning Associates released a study recommending preservation on the west side of Columbia Road. It said that historic buildings should be saved, renovated and reused. The city should not compete with Great Northern or Berea's commercial district by seeking chain stores, the report said. Instead, Olmsted Falls should attract specialty shops to combine "historical significance and economic vitality." The area included was south of the railroad tracks, west of Columbia Road, north of Bagley Road and east of Brookside Drive.

In 1978, Clint Williams received city permission to turn a former gas station at the northwestern corner of Columbia Road and Water Street into an office for his real estate business. The gas station had been built in 1926 at the site where Chauncey Mead had operated a harness shop in the 1800s. Gordon Schady operated it as a Shell station from 1935 to 1965. Williams had to clear regulatory obstacles, but the result was a renovation that fit with the character of the community. In 1981, the Cleveland Area Board of Realtors gave the building a Medallion Home Award for helping to "preserve, protect and upgrade the real estate market."

About the same time, the city converted a former residence at the corner of Columbia Road and Main Street, just south of the library, into a multipurpose community center. It opened in May 1981 as the Jenkins Center, named after William Jenkins, a community leader who had served as councilman and municipal clerk. He died in 1973 at age seventy-five.

TOWNSHIP DEVELOPMENTS

In the township, the intersection of Bagley and Stearns Roads became an entertainment center in the 1980s. First, businessman Fred Shaker, owner of Shaker's IGA grocery, opened the Golden Tee Driving Range in 1980. In 1987, Tim Sorge opened Swings-N-Things with miniature golf and batting cages. It eventually included bumper boats, go-carts, a game arcade and facilities for paintball and laser tag competition.

Financial problems in township government led to the resignation early in 1981 of Bernice Loudermilk as township clerk, a position she had held for nine years. The county prosecutor sued her because more than $142,000 in township funds was missing. In April 1983, she was sentenced to four to fifteen years in prison, as the *News Sun* reported, after she pleaded "guilty to 56 counts of forgery and theft in office…The total amount of money taken [over a period of several years] by the former clerk [represented] about one-third of Olmsted Township's annual budget." Loudermilk was released after serving less than three years in the Marysville Reformatory.

During the 1980s, the former Ritter Farm at 7370 Columbia Road underwent transformation. A German heritage group, the Donauschwabens—or Danube Swabians—bought twenty acres in 1970 for sports and cultural activities. Initially, they used the old farmhouse as a clubhouse. But during the 1980s, they built a large cultural center with a gym, dance halls and meeting spaces. The Ritter farmhouse was torn down in 1992.

Another development transformed Homelinks Golf Course. In 1984, the Eliza Jennings Foundation announced plans to establish a retirement community called the Renaissance with a one-million-gallon lake and a redesigned golf course. The Eliza Jennings Corporation bought the 164 acres from Homelinks, Inc., by the end of 1985. In June 1986, Willard Scott, the weatherman on NBC-TV's *Today* show, helped break ground. By early 1989, the first residents had moved in.

Land Grabs

The township again became a target for annexation attempts, some successful, in the 1980s. The township and Olmsted Falls considered and then fought over proposals to attach the entire township to the city.

In 1986, a group of businesspeople along a 1.3-mile, 290-acre Bagley Road strip between Olmsted Falls and Berea set off competition between the two cities to annex that portion of the township. They wanted water and sewer service. The township fought any loss of territory. Trustee Robert Stackhouse called the strip "a plum everyone wants." At one point, the property owners leaned toward joining Olmsted Falls, but Berea mayor John Whipple made a more persuasive case. Berea already had a wastewater treatment plant, but Olmsted Falls was still planning one. Berea won. The county commissioners approved the annexation in late March 1987. Six months later, Berea formally accepted the land. The corridor remained within the Olmsted Falls City School District so property taxes continued to benefit the schools. But Berea received the rest of the tax benefits from the light industrial and commercial operations that developed.

In July 1989, Brook Park emerged as a suitor for township land. Among the township's neighbors, Brook Park had the smallest border with it—all of it along the Rocky River in the Metroparks system. Mayor Thomas Coyne promised lower taxes, better services and a recreation center. He said he wanted the township for housing, not industrial development. Some township residents liked the proposal. Others stepped up merger talks with Olmsted Falls. By that fall, North Olmsted and Berea had also expressed interest in township land. Township trustees even considered incorporation again.

By November 1991, a proposal to form a commission to work on a Falls-township merger had appeared on the ballot. City voters overwhelmingly approved it; township voters narrowly rejected it—the second such rejection in four years.

RENEWAL

1990–2010

Olmsted underwent significant transformation in the 1990s. It could have happened on the edges, considering all the proposals to attach all or part of the township to neighboring communities. Instead, it happened in the middle, not by change but by preservation.

In January 1990, real estate company owner Clint Williams revealed plans to renovate several of the oldest buildings in the center of Olmsted Falls. He had bought the two acres they stood on in late 1989.

But it almost did not happen. Several years earlier, Williams had worked out the deal for a National City Bank branch to displace what had been Simmerer & Sons' Hardware and later Kucklick's Village Square Shoppe Annex. If that had happened, the whole block might have been redeveloped much like Mill River Plaza across the street. Later, Williams showed the property to other potential buyers until he saw the buildings in a new light.

"I stood down on this corner of Orchard Street and Mill," he said in 2004. "I really hadn't paid that much attention to it before, but it just kind of struck me as an old-fashioned town. Then I said, 'Maybe I ought to buy it and restore one at a time.'"

The property was bordered by Columbia Road on the east, Mill Street on the south, Plum Creek on the west and the railroad tracks on the north. Williams wanted to put retail stores, professional offices, an upscale restaurant and perhaps a bed-and-breakfast in the buildings.

The initial response from some city officials and residents was positive, but the proposal got bogged down in several months of disputes, mainly over parking. Mill River Development, owner of the shopping center across the street, fought the zoning board's attempt to give Williams a variance. That variance would allow the project to proceed with only 95 parking spaces instead of the 167 spaces called for in the zoning code. Mill River protested that its parking lot would get the spillover.

"I finally said, 'To hell with it,' and I just started to work on it," Williams said, although he had to scale the project down a bit. "We put in nineteen merchants in twenty-four months. I guess you have to appreciate the fact that we had no city sewers, so sewer just came in then. We had to put sewers to all these buildings, electrical, gas, all new furnaces, all new air-conditioning."

In the fall of 1990, Williams named the project Grand Pacific Junction. That was after the Grand Pacific Hotel, the name he returned to the former hardware store when he restored it to the way it looked in the 1800s.

"Olmsted Falls didn't have a downtown," Williams said.

> *It was gone. So this created first a downtown for the people to come and sit and browse and eat an ice cream cone—whatever they want to do. I think the reason it worked was because of the fact there are flat storefronts like in the late 1800s, there are Victorian homes and the hotel…And then, there's always been an ambience about this place. When you walk through it, you get a feeling.*

In the restoration process, he made a few changes to increase the usefulness of the buildings for retail operations, such as lengthening the old jail and moving it and the former carriage house to new locations. But otherwise, Williams kept as many features—such as hinges, latches and other hardware—as possible. He tore the enclosed stairway off the side of the Grand Pacific Hotel because it was not an original part of the building.

One of the hardest buildings for Williams to convert was the L-shaped Depositors Bank Building; not the front facing Columbia Road—it already had well-defined storefronts—but the side extending 160 feet back from the street.

"So I said, 'Let's do a boardwalk,'" Williams said. "I wanted to keep it in a sense the Wild West theme, something that would be out of the past, so to speak. So we came up with the different roof lines and added a second story. Then we put a porch over the whole thing."

Fitting with the theme, he added a gazebo overlooking Plum Creek and parked a 1922 Vulcan locomotive and a red caboose next to it. Over the years, Williams restored other buildings as part of Grand Pacific Junction, including the Grange Hall, the former Fenderbosch Saloon, the Wedding

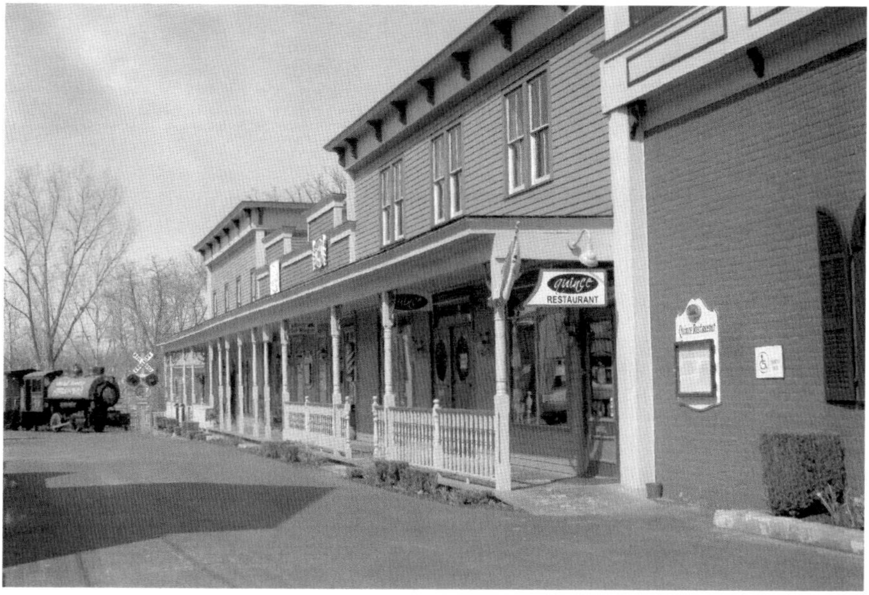

Clint Williams created more storefronts by opening up the south side of the Depositors Bank Building. *Photo by Jim Wallace.*

Chapel, the Bonsey Building and an 1895 train depot. He has received several awards for the Grand Pacific Junction renovations.

In 1992, Williams was instrumental in starting the annual Olmsted Heritage Days festival based at Grand Pacific Junction.

Park Improvements

Grand Pacific Junction was the biggest change to Olmsted's appearance in the 1990s but not the only one. In the mid-'90s, Olmsted Falls created East River Park. For years, the city had owned five acres of undeveloped land along the east bank of the Rocky River across from David Fortier River Park. In 1987, the city bought a one-hundred- by five-hundred-foot parcel for access from Lewis Road. Work began on an entrance drive and parking lot in 1994. A $162,000 state grant in 1995 went along with about $78,000 a year from a one-mill recreation levy to pay for the improvements, including a picnic pavilion, picnic tables, hiking trails and playground equipment. Volunteers helped complete some of that work in 1996.

A few years later, another park was improved. The city built a brick pavilion on the Village Green, which gave an old school bell a new home. The bell was from the Union Schoolhouse that stood there until 1960. The pavilion was designed to somewhat resemble the old school with the bell at the top.

Another significant improvement came in 1998 with the installation of a covered wooden bridge on Main Street over Plum Creek. It replaced an iron trestle that the county had built in 1905. The city closed that bridge in 1981 after a thirteen-thousand-pound truck crossed it, ignoring a load limit sign. The bridge already had been deteriorating, and city officials feared it was no longer safe for any vehicular traffic. For years, the community considered several proposals to replace it. None went very far until 1995, when a plan emerged for the pedestrian-only wooden bridge. The Kiwanis Club of Olmsted Falls set up a nonprofit corporation, the Olmsted Falls Kiwanis Civic Development Foundation, to coordinate the project. Fundraising efforts included the sale of $50 and $100 memorial bricks on the walkway to the bridge. The foundation also received $125,000 in state funds and a substantial donation from Amelia and Clara Harding, who were fourth-generation Olmsted Falls residents. The bridge was named the Charles A. Harding Memorial Bridge after the Harding sisters' brother, who died on August 3, 1944, from wounds suffered in the Battle of Normandy in World War II.

Construction began in April 1998. On June 25, 1998, a group of Amish workers rolled the bridge, made of red oak and cedar, into place and then installed the flooring. It was 108 feet long, 90 feet of which went over Plum Creek. The cost was almost $400,000. The city opened the bridge in a dedication ceremony on August 9, 1998.

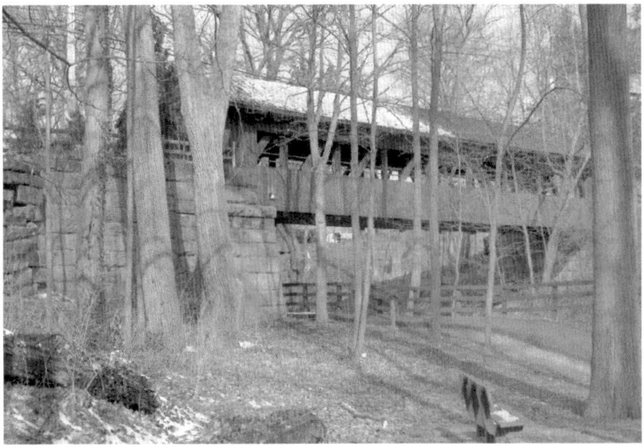

Since 1998, the Charles A. Harding Memorial Bridge has been one of the most photographed sites in Olmsted Falls. *Photo by Jim Wallace.*

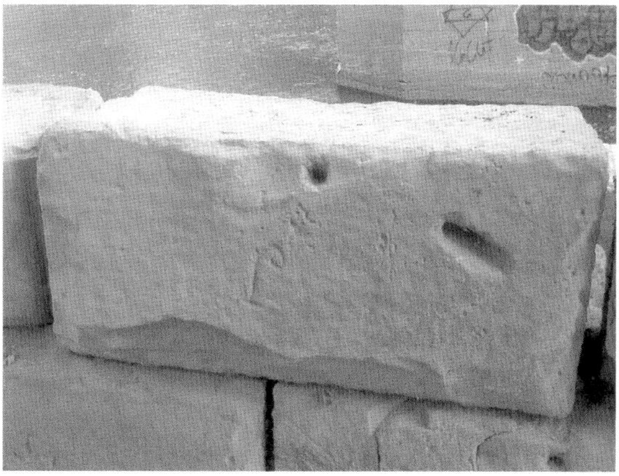

Builders of the new Water Street Bridge in 1990 were persuaded not to destroy what remains of one of three stone columns that held up the 1864 bridge wrecked by the 1913 flood. Some stones bear unusual letter-like markings that were apparently symbols of their makers. *Photo by Bruce Banks.*

Other Bridges

Less photogenic bridges also were built during the 1990s. Water Street's bridge over the Rocky River was replaced in 1990. A state agency had declared the old bridge among the twenty worst bridges in a five-county region. But the new bridge's concrete sides disappointed many people because motorists could no longer view the waterfalls on the river.

In November 1994, a new $3.4 million bridge to carry Bagley Road over the Rocky River opened after more than a decade of planning and ten months of construction. It was part of a larger project to expand Bagley Road from two lanes to four lanes from the railroad tracks in Berea to Columbia Road in Olmsted Falls.

At the southern end of Olmsted Falls, on Sprague Road, another two-lane bridge over the Rocky River was replaced with a four-lane bridge. After eight months of construction, the new bridge opened in November 1998 at a cost of about $2 million.

In the northern part of the township, the county completely rebuilt John Road early in the 1990s to expand its width from twenty to twenty-eight feet with concrete pavement, curbs, storm drains and sidewalks. The cost was more than $2 million.

New School, Old School

Another construction project in the township was the new $15 million middle school built west of the high school on Bagley Road. It opened in November 1997. For the first time in more than eighty years, the 1916 school, which once housed all of the district's classes, was no longer needed as a school. There was much debate over what to do with it. One possibility was to move the public library into it. Another was to tear it down.

Instead, the school district sold the property in October 1997 to FirstNorth Development Corp. for $225,000. One year later, the city bought the building's oldest section and 1.9 acres around it for use as a new city hall. The city paid $125,000 for the building and another $125,000 for FirstNorth's help preparing it to hold city offices, including the police department. For years, city officials had wanted to replace North Hall and South Hall, which predated the Olmsted Falls–West View merger. Their total fourteen thousand square feet was one-third of the old school's space. The old gym and cafeteria became a community center. The building's western wing became a day-care center.

TOWNSHIP TURF BATTLES

After losing more than five hundred acres to annexation in the 1980s, the township trustees made a brief attempt at incorporation in 1990. But the 1990s mostly were filled with more attempts by neighboring cities to get township land.

After taking over the Bagley Road corridor in the 1980s, Berea wanted more land east of the river. Under a 1995 plan, Berea would have taken the whole eastern section, and North Olmsted would have taken everything west of the river and north of the Ohio Turnpike. A citizens' group called the Future of Olmsted Township (FOOT) favored merging the township with Brook Park. Other citizens favored merger with Olmsted Falls, which had the most in common with the township.

Most efforts did not go far, but a 1992 proposal to annex 195 acres to Berea raged for several years until an appeals court rejected it in 2000.

JEDD

Beginning in 1999, Olmsted Falls and the township, along with the school district, began a joint effort to improve their industrial base. With little industry to tax, the school district's residential property tax burden was about 50 percent above the state average. Using a 1993 state law, officials created the Joint Economic Development District (JEDD) in 2001. It would allow the city to provide water and sewer service to a township industrial zone. The township would impose an income tax on workers in that zone to repay the city for infrastructure costs.

In 2004, a consulting company estimated that the JEDD could create forty-eight hundred jobs and $51 million in tax revenue, although it would take a few decades to develop. In 2006, the JEDD proposed using 243 acres between Bagley, Stearns, Cook and Bronson Roads with potential expansion to another 142 acres.

Off Track

Even while officials worked to attract more industry, the township lost a tourist attraction. The Brookins family sold Columbia Mobile Home Park in 2001. The new owner had no interest in keeping Trolleyville, USA. A nonprofit group, Lake Shore Electric Railway Inc., bought the trolleys and planned to run them on a downtown Cleveland loop near a trolley museum. But the plan fell through. The organization auctioned off the trolleys in 2009. All that is left of Trolleyville in Olmsted is the former Baltimore & Ohio Railroad depot that Clint Williams moved in 2008 to Grand Pacific Junction.

A township improvement project also went awry. Township officials planned to build much-needed new facilities for the police, fire and service departments financed with $2.8 million in bonds. In October 2005, the new $1 million police station opened. But within a year, construction on the partially completed fire station and service garage halted because of financial troubles. One trustee blamed another for negotiating contracts that gave contractors too much leeway, turning a $2.8 million project into $3.6 million of obligations. Those contractors sued or threatened to sue until the trustees dug into various funds for $317,000 to pay six of them off in 2007.

More Welcome Construction

Another construction project in the township fared better. In August 2009, the school system opened a new $16.6 million intermediate school for fourth and fifth graders. It was built next to the middle school on Bagley Road.

In 2010, work began on a long-awaited project in Olmsted Falls: the construction of an underpass so Columbia Road traffic would no longer have to cross the CSX Transportation railroad tracks near Sprague Road.

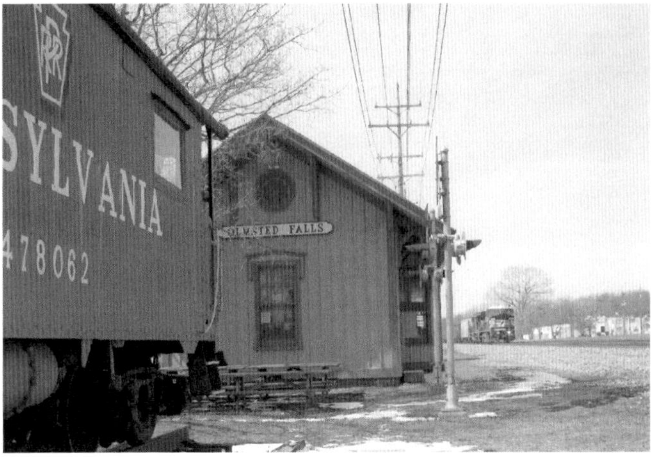

Traffic from trains, such as this one passing the 1876 Olmsted Falls depot, increased after 1998, leading to efforts to create a "quiet zone." *Photo by Jim Wallace.*

That was part of an overall plan to improve safety and cut down on train noise. Also planned were overpasses on Fitch and Stearns Roads to replace the Norfolk Southern track crossings.

The underpass and overpass projects, along with safety upgrades at other crossings, would permit establishment of a "quiet zone" under a 2004 Ohio law. Trains were such an irritant in Olmsted that Governor Bob Taft signed the quiet zone bill into law in a ceremony at Grand Pacific Junction. Although blocked crossings and noisy trains had been problems for decades, the situation got worse after CSX and Norfolk Southern acquired Conrail in 1998. Traffic on the CSX tracks increased from about fifteen trains a day previously to about sixty in 2000. On the Norfolk Southern tracks, traffic increased to about seventy-four trains a day in 2005. In a quiet zone, trains would not have to blow their horns at all hours day and night as they approach crossings.

Annexation Expectations

Proposals to change the status of the township came up again early in the twenty-first century. In 2009, voters had a chance to approve a study of a Falls-township merger and to set up a commission to conduct that study. City voters strongly supported it. Township voters narrowly opposed it.

If the future is consistent with the past, annexation efforts will continue as long as there is a township.

THE WORK OF OLMSTED

Industry—and sometimes the lack of it—shaped life in Olmsted.

Agriculture was the pioneers' first industry. James Geer, the township's first settler, grew corn on a small piece of Olmsted land in 1814, a year before he and his family moved into the township. Other early Olmsted residents also had to live off of the land. In 1870, L.B. Adams wrote in Berea's *Grindstone City Advertiser* that Olmsted was "a fine farming region, high and dry with good air and water." Articles mentioned many crops, including wheat, corn, oats, hay, potatoes, apples, peaches, grapes and several kinds of berries. In 1885, the *Berea Advertiser* called D.K. Huntington of the Butternut Ridge area "the leader of North Olmsted in growing small fruit, he having about thirty acres of strawberries, blackberries, raspberries, and currants in bearing." In addition to crops, Olmsted's farmers raised livestock, including sheep, goats, hogs, cows, chickens and turkeys.

Many other enterprises, such as cheese factories, were related to agriculture. For example, Richard Carpenter, with help from his brother, established a cheese factory at Butternut Ridge in 1870. In April 1873, the *Advertiser* noted that cheese making was about to begin for the season at Carpenter's factory "on a larger scale than last year. Jonathan Carpenter & Son have fifty cows of their own and intend to manufacture their own cheese. The dairy business seems to be on the increase in this vicinity." Cheese factories also operated in Olmsted Falls and other parts of the township.

Mills

An area producing wheat and other grains needed to process that grain into flour. Thus, some of the earliest industrial operations in Olmsted were the gristmills, as well as sawmills, established by such early settlers as Lemuel Hoadley, John Barnum and Watrous Usher to take advantage of the flowing waters of the Rocky River and Plum Creek.

Lemuel Hoadley's brother, Calvin, built the first gristmill in Columbia Township in 1809 along the west branch of the Rocky River toward the center of that township. Later that year, Calvin and Lemuel built a gristmill and sawmill farther north on the river, just south of what became Olmsted Township. That area was called West View, reportedly because of the view to the west that Calvin had from his home (where Riverside Golf Course was built later). West View straddled the border of Lorain and Cuyahoga Counties (although the Village of West View incorporated in the twentieth century was entirely on the Olmsted side of the line).

Thomas Chambers, an English miller who moved to America in 1870, bought Hoadleys' Mill in 1882. In March 1883, a great flood severely damaged the mill, but Chambers rebuilt it and upgraded it. He rebuilt it again after another great flood, in March 1913, also damaged the mill. Chambers operated it until 1920. (Almost a century later, stones from the mill's dam can still be seen in the river south of the Sprague Road Bridge. Gibbs Butcher Block, a meat market and gourmet grocery, occupies the site in a building similar to the old mill.)

Lemuel Hoadley also built a sawmill near Cedar Point in northeastern Olmsted Township. John Barnum worked for him there and married his

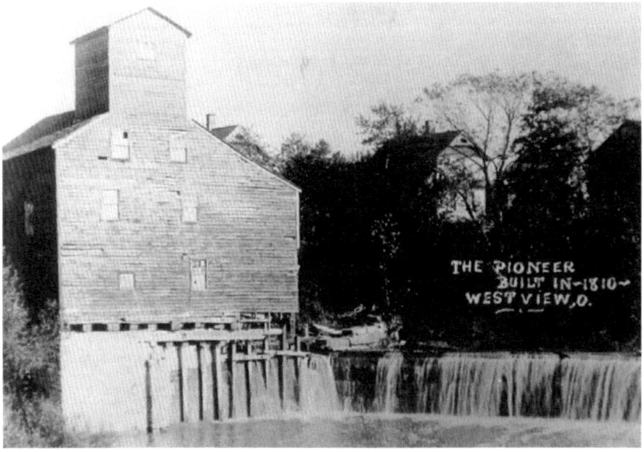

The early nineteenth-century mill built by the Hoadley brothers remained an important business on Olmsted Township's southern border for many decades.

daughter, Eunice. In 1832, Hoadley and Barnum built another sawmill along Plum Creek, near its mouth. (A careful observer still can see a diagonal line on the side of Inscription Rock in what is now David Fortier River Park. It apparently shows where Hoadley and Barnum anchored planks of wood for their dam across the creek. Square holes and other cutouts in the rock creek bed also seem to reveal where the dam was anchored. A hand-chiseled channel next to the creek appears to have been a sluice for the mill, which probably used an undershot wheel.)

Watrous Usher, who came to Olmsted (then Lenox) Township in 1820, built sawmills on Plum Creek and on a creek near Bodecker Hill (by what is now Columbia Road in North Olmsted).

More than one mill was built next to the waterfalls along Plum Creek (near where the present Dan Waugh Nature Trail looks out over the falls) in the center of Olmsted Falls. Newton Loomis, whose 1834 home is now used as the public library, is credited with building the first mill there. Sometime around 1870, two Alcott brothers, Sylvester and Levi, built a sawmill there. The mill became known as the Alcott and Stokes Mill after Tom Stokes joined the business. An 1873 newspaper account noted they had a lumberyard, as well as "a planing and matching machine, and intend to do their work in a satisfactory manner." In the autumn, they also pressed apples from an orchard at the corner of what is now Brookside Drive and Elm Street into cider. In 1878, they produced more than two thousand barrels of

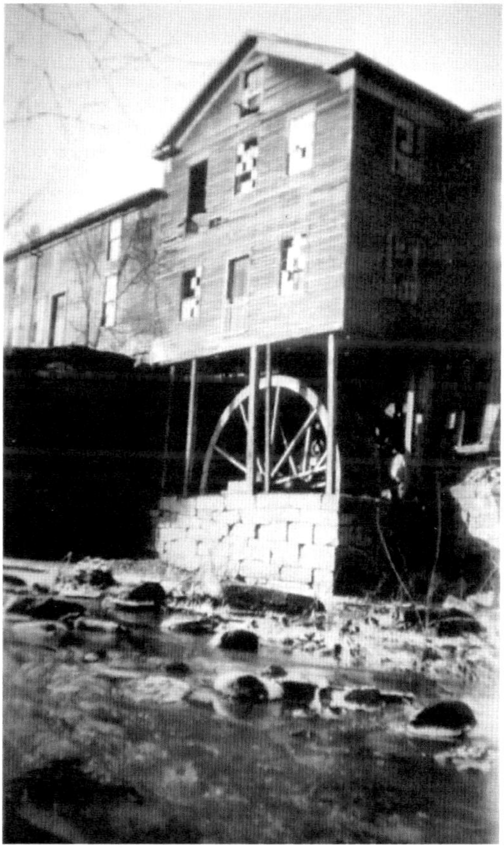

The mill of Tom Stokes once towered over the Plum Creek waterfalls. Part of the mill's stone foundation is still there.

cider. In 1883, Stokes bought out Alcott's interest and operated the business on his own.

In 1982, Charles Bonsey, who played near there as a boy, described the planing mill: "They made finished lumber out of rough lumber. We used to go down and watch the planer. It made a fascinating noise. The knives would spin around and would throw out little shavings."

Stokes lived in a house next to the mill. In 1887, he built a big building next to it to store lumber and other material from the mill. He also was a proud veteran of the Civil War. The local chapter of the veterans' organization, the Grand Army of the Republic, was formed about the time his building was completed, so he let the post use the second floor for meetings. Thus, it became known as the GAR Hall. (That building still exists as a residence at 7835 Columbia Road.)

Along Rocky River next to the Olmsted Falls business district, Colonel H.N. Whitbeck began operating a gristmill at least by 1870. The April 8, 1870 edition of the *Advertiser* included the following item:

> *Among the late improvements of our village, we are glad to notice that Col. H.N. Whitbeck has made a thorough overhauling and general fixing up of his flouring mill, introducing a new corncracker, and Empire corn sheller, new belts, etc. He intends to make his mill second to none in the country.*

But Whitbeck apparently fell short of such hopes, judging by an August 29, 1873 item: "The grist mill has changed hands again. Perhaps it will fall into the right man's hands sometime."

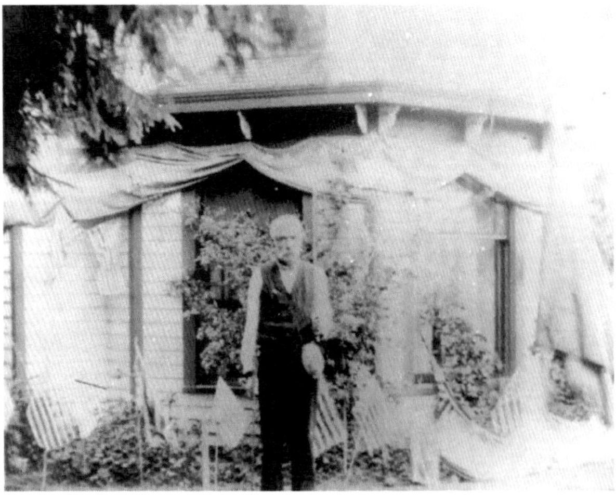

Tom Stokes was a patriotic Civil War veteran who helped form the Olmsted post of the Grand Army of the Republic.

The right man apparently was Ed Damp, who operated the mill, sometimes with partners as Damp & Difford or Damp Brothers, for three decades beginning in the mid-1870s. The mill's dam backed up so much water that it turned the Rocky River at that point into a pond, which local residents used for recreational boating in the summer and ice skating in the winter. A March 1883 flood damaged the mill and its foundation badly. Damp rebuilt it in the same spot with a thirteen-foot-high stone foundation topped with two stories of wooden structure. Damp sold the mill in 1906.

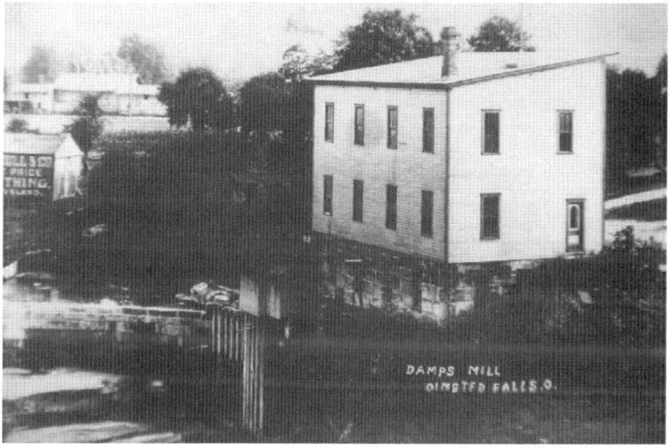

Right: After the 1883 flood, Ed Damp had local stone mason Joseph Gibson rebuild his mill bigger than before.

Below: The mill owned by Thomas Chambers at West View survived the 1913 flood, but the Sprague Road Bridge was washed away.

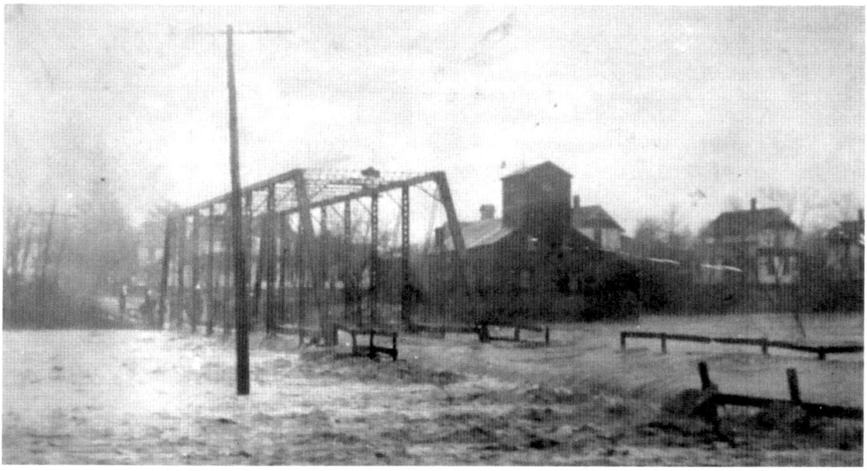

"We used to watch the mill go around, shell the corn and grind feed for farmers and flour," Bonsey recalled. "I think you could go down there and buy a sack of flour wholesale." He also remembered a fanning mill:

> *When farmers brought wheat to be ground, sometimes it would have a lot of chaff in it. They'd have to remove the chaff from the wheat. There was a certain machine that did that. The chaff would go into one place and the pure wheat would come out another place.*

Another big flood on March 28, 1913, ruined most of the mill. All but the foundation's stone walls was torn down later.

Although early mills were located along Plum Creek or the Rocky River to take advantage of flowing water, some Olmsted residents in the 1800s used steam-powered sawmills in the woods.

TOOLS, FELLOES, BROOMS, BRICKS, PAINT AND COFFINS

Peter Kidney, who came to Olmsted in 1833, established a sawmill and a gristmill near what is now River Road. He also established a factory to make sharp-edged tools using a triphammer and local sandstone. Later, he manufactured cheese boxes and other wooden items, including buckets, measures and chairs.

Kidney's son, Edward, set up Kidney Bending Works (also called Cleveland Bending Works), which made bows for buggy tops, felloes (wheel rims) and other curved parts for wagons. At its peak, the factory on the west side of what is now River Road employed a few dozen men. In 1886, it added a night shift to keep up with business. A fire destroyed the factory in 1890, but Kidney reestablished it with two buildings, one fifty-four by forty feet with two stories and another forty by eighty feet. He also started making bicycle wheel rims. In addition to operating the bending works, Kidney invented and marketed a water filter for many years.

Charles Bonsey recalled seeing a big team of horses hauling wagonloads of logs from the railroad station to the bending works. "They cut the logs up down there into strips that would be about one-by-two," he said.

> *Somehow, they had some kind of machine that shaved the corners off so that they were rounded. There was a big steam oven that they put this*

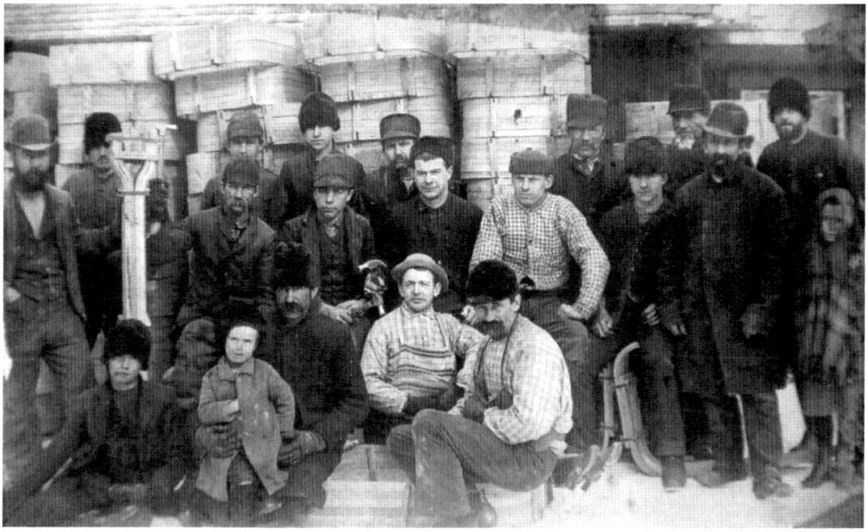

Ed Kidney sits in front of workers at his bending works in Olmsted Falls.

> *lumber in. They cut them into strips about ten feet long. They would have ten to twelve of those made…The ten sticks were fastened together by strips of wood, and they put them into the steam oven to make them pliable. Then they would take them out of the steam oven, put them on a flat table, a heavy metal table, and the strips of wood would be fastened down rigid. And the ends would come up by power and bend them. Then they would put strips across to hold them in that position until they dried. Then they could take the fasteners off. I can remember they would put two of these together that made a piece of wood, and they would ship them.*

Those buggy bows would be sent down a sawdust-covered chute to a wagon that would take them, piled five to six feet high, to the depot to be shipped by railroad to a buggy factory.

In 1901, Kidney moved to Memphis, Tennessee, to run another company's bending works. His former partner, Gus Leutkemeyer, dismantled the factory and shipped much of its equipment to a similar factory in Metropolis, Illinois. Kidney returned to Olmsted Falls in 1904 and lived there until 1920.

Another industrious family were the Lays, who arrived in the 1850s. John and Joseph Lay built a factory near Kidney's factory to make wooden rakes, scythes and other farm implements. They also built wagon parts and cheese boxes. Later, Joseph took over the factory—then called Joseph Lay & Co.—and

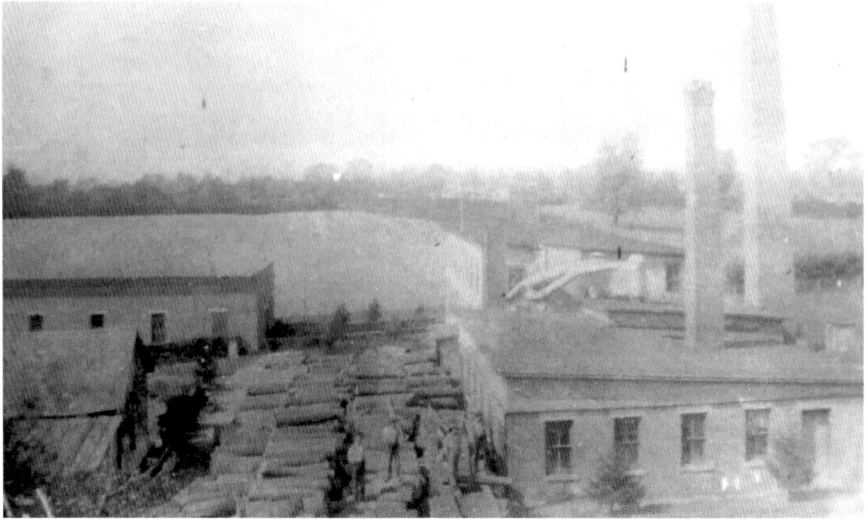

The bending works had a big factory off of Bradford Road (now River Road).

used it to make brooms and snow shovels. Even though the factory suffered fire and flood, it kept going. In November 1885, the company was reported to be so busy that despite having the employees "working night and day they are not able to fill their orders" for brooms and snow shovels. In 1897, Joseph moved to Ridgeville, Indiana, to run the Crescent Co., which was called the country's largest broom factory. Several Olmsted residents followed him there.

An area near where the current River Road meets Nobottom Road was the site, in the mid-1800s, of a brick factory run by brothers Lester and Eastman Bradford. (Chips of red brick can still be found in the ground there. They also can be found in the ground in David Fortier River Park north of Plum Creek and west of Rocky River. Apparently, the bricks were used to rebuild Lemuel Hoadley's mill after it burned down.) The bricks were hand-packed with no holes in them and fired in the Bradfords' kiln. Each one was about four inches by six inches by two inches.

Other Olmsted buildings in the 1800s also had a reddish brown color from paint made from shale found along Minnie Creek (which flows below Columbia Road near All Saints Lutheran Church). The shale was ground into a powder and mixed with oil and turpentine at a paint factory built there by Philo, Myron and Lester Bradford in 1848. "We manufactured paint for two and a half years, taking it from the bank in crude form," Lester Bradford recalled in 1882, when he was sixty-three. "My two brothers, Myron and

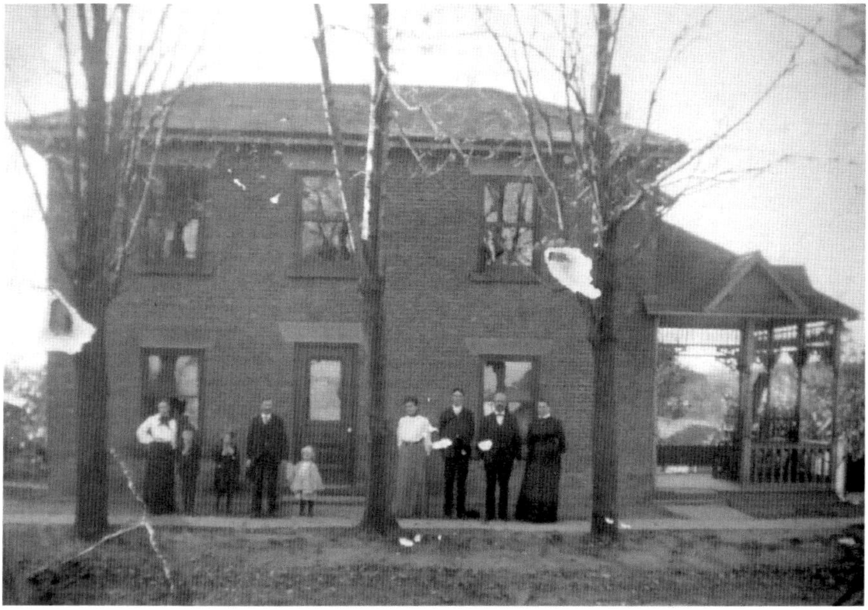

Bradford bricks were used to build the house at 8008 Columbia Road.

Hiram, died of consumption, caused by working in the paint mill." Lester Bradford also operated a sawmill at that spot for ten years. (The building at 7990–7994 Columbia Road, which was the Fenderbosch Saloon and Pool Hall—now Master Cleaners and the Olde Wine Cellar—is believed to be painted a color similar to the old pigment made by the Bradfords.)

Along Butternut Ridge, John Ames operated a coffin factory and did other woodwork in a two-story building that previously served as both a church and a town hall (Town House Corners). That was a good location for making coffins because it was close to the Butternut Ridge Cemetery, where many of Olmsted's early residents were buried.

Quarries

Olmsted's biggest industry in the last few decades of the 1800s was quarrying sandstone. The Olmsted Falls and West View quarries contained Berea Grit, the same type of sandstone quarried in Berea since the 1830s.

The sandstone was used for grindstones, building blocks and sidewalks. The quarries started in the 1870s, although some West View residents found quarry work in the 1860s at Baxter Clough's quarry in Columbia Township, just south of West View. Because of quarrying, the railroad upgraded its West View station, as the newspaper reported on July 29, 1870: "The railroad company is putting up a new depot building at this station—they have already put in some large scales for weighing stone."

About quarrying in Olmsted Falls, the *Advertiser* reported in May 1871:

> *The stone business is on the increase in our village. The Lake Huron Stone Co., under the superintendence of O.W. Kendall, has made a beginning and expects soon to employ forty men. This company is now putting in an engine. Pelper & Perkins employ about fifteen men. McDonald, Barnum and House are running a good business with seventy men; they have lately put in steam power.*

By August 1871, the number of laborers in Olmsted's quarries had more than tripled—or "trebled" as the *Advertiser* put it. Another Olmsted item from August 1872 noted, "The firm of Wallace & Russell have commenced work in their new quarry and have shipped some block

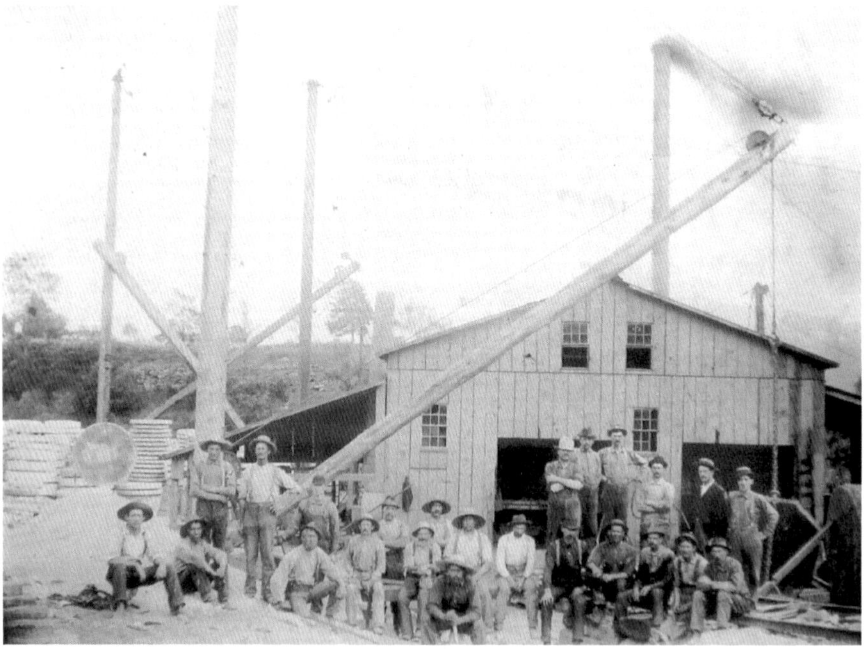

This and other quarrying operations changed the contours of the land that became David Fortier River Park, named after an Olmsted Falls mayor killed in a 1986 car crash.

stone." That quarry, in September 1873, then called Wallace and Baker's, made a huge grindstone weighing 7,972 pounds. In November 1885, Jeremiah LeDuke opened a new quarry with about $20,000 worth of machinery near Plum Creek in Olmsted Falls. The stone business even reached Butternut Ridge when Edmund Stearns opened a quarry there early in 1886.

"The success of the quarries means good times for Olmsted," the *Advertiser* reported in 1885. "Mr. L. Barnum can hardly keep pace with orders for grindstone."

An *Advertiser* article in November 1875 reported that quarrymen at West View's Rocky River Stone Co. were

> *pushing their work along at a brisk and lively rate in getting out grindstones, which are said to be equal if not superior to any stone now in the market by those that have used them...They cannot supply the demand for their blue stone for grinding. They are running one large lathe and will put in another one this month for small stone.*

Charles Bonsey, whose father had worked in the quarries, said in 1982 that an upright lathe was used to make grindstones:

> *The stone would be lifted with a derrick into this lathe, and of course, it was tightened with a big screw and a big nut, something like that, and then the machinery would turn the stone slowly. He had some sort of a bar across that he made tension—a bar with some sort of an end that was fat...He'd hold that on the stone, and there was some way he moved it from side to side to make the stone even and grind it down to a smooth surface.*

But quarrying was dangerous. On April 4, 1878, the *Advertiser* reported a serious accident at West View's Rocky River Stone quarry:

> *There are two derricks which stand in front of the mill that are fastened together by a guy, reaching from one to the other, another guy leads from one of the derricks to a tree to which it is fastened. While engaged in hoisting a stone the guy which led to the tree broke lose* [sic]*, and both derricks fell, one of the guys striking George Boon in the side and, it was thought at first, breaking several ribs. Dr. Rose, of Olmsted Falls, was sent for who pronounced one of his ribs broken and one cracked.*

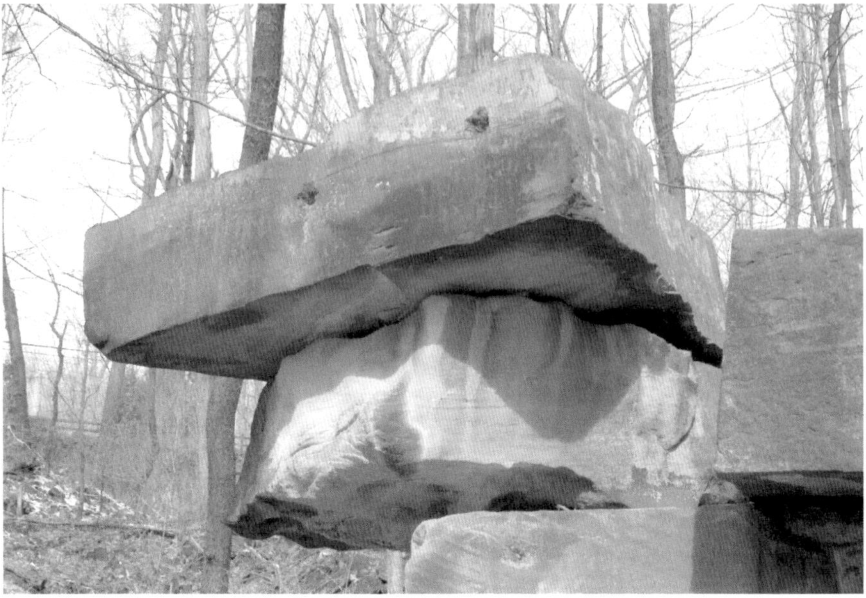

Piles of big stones from the quarries remain in the park in Olmsted Falls. *Photo by Jim Wallace.*

Two weeks later, another accident there involved a train pulled by a small "pony engine" locomotive. The engine was hauling cars from the quarry, the newspaper reported,

> *when the tender jumped the track and fell on its side. The engine jumped the track also, but did not fall over…The track for the space of fifteen or twenty feet was torn up and a number of the rails were bent. No one was hurt, although the engineer and fireman had a narrow escape.*

Luther Barnum twice almost lost his life in his Olmsted Falls quarry. In September 1871, he dropped a lighted match into a powder keg he thought was empty. But it still had powder clinging to its side. The subsequent explosion burned off his heavy beard, scorched his skin and initially made it difficult for him to see and breathe. "The force of the powder may be judged from the fact that a large hole was blown in the crown of Mr. B's hat," the *Advertiser* reported.

In August 1882, when Barnum was mayor, a hook raising a stone slipped. Barnum was struck in the head and knocked unconscious, but he recovered.

Quarrying also caused silicosis, an irreversible disease from inhaling silica dust. Quarrymen called it "grit consumption." Silicosis damages a person's lungs with such symptoms as chest pain, fatigue, shortness of breath and fever.

The formation of the Cleveland Stone Company by George H. Worthington in 1886 ended the days of quarries operated separately by individual owners. The company acquired quarries in Olmsted Falls, West View, Berea, Columbia, Elyria, Euclid, Kipton, North Amherst, South Amherst and LaGrange. The company boasted of supplying construction stones for Canada's Parliament in Ottawa, the Hancock Building in Boston and the Palmer House Hotel in Chicago, among others.

In 1888, Cleveland Stone built a new railroad spur for its Olmsted Falls quarry. It began near the depot, crossed Main Street (now Columbia Road) and then crossed Plum Creek on a trestle near the falls. Trestle support beams were anchored in square-cut holes in the stone creek bed upstream from the falls. (Those holes are still there.) The track then went along the top of the steep bank south of the creek to the quarry.

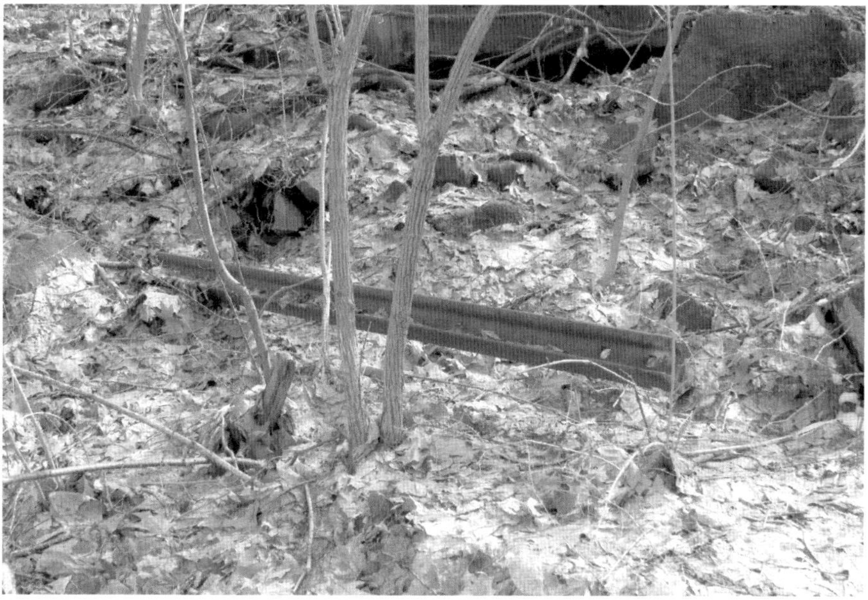

A former spur track rail pokes out of stones in David Fortier River Park. Another protrudes from the base of a tree along Rocky River just north of Plum Creek. Much of the track bed has become a trail that passes under the Charles A. Harding Memorial Bridge. *Photo by Jim Wallace.*

However, Olmsted residents became disillusioned with Cleveland Stone. In November 1888, the company cut quarrymen's pay to one dollar. "Many refuse to work for these wages," the *Advertiser* reported. Village residents already were upset that the railroad tore up the street for months to build the spur and for months afterward. In August 1889, some workers were reported leaving the West View quarries for better jobs in Colorado. When wages again dropped in December 1891, it was reported that "a number of the hands left for their homes in different parts of the country."

Like most companies, Cleveland Stone suffered from the Panic of 1893, a steep economic downturn that caused about fifteen thousand companies nationwide to fail and unemployment to climb. Cleveland Stone kept going but with another reduction in workers' pay.

By 1896, many Cleveland Stone quarrymen had become dissatisfied, especially after workers in other trades had their wages restored to pre-1893 levels. Many quarrymen joined a union, the Knights of Labor. On May 12, the union local at Berea presented demands, including the rehiring of union members discharged by the company, restoration of the 10 percent of wages cut from workers' pay two years earlier and annual wage negotiations. The company refused.

On June 11, most Berea quarrymen went on strike. A small number of nonunion men remained working. The union held daily mass meetings, attended by quarrymen and their wives.

The strike soon spread to fourteen Cleveland Stone quarries, but the Olmsted Falls correspondent for the *Advertiser* reported in mid-June:

> *Again the desire for better wages has manifested itself in the quarrymen of Berea, and they tried to induce our men to join in the strike, but of no avail. The leaders were not gifted sufficiently in the use of the American language to convince Foreman Barnum and his faithful loyal men that their actions were in accordance with the views of Uncle Sam, even if they did carry "Old Glory" in the lead. We are yet a firm believer in the motto of that noble order that should be thoroughly organized in every hamlet, the Jr. OUAM…"America for Americans."*

By mentioning the Junior Order of United American Mechanics, an anti-immigrant organization, the correspondent revealed antipathy to the many eastern Europeans who worked in the quarries.

By June 18, an estimated sixteen hundred men were on strike. Sheriff F.W. Leek deputized more than one hundred men. Two National Guard units were called out to maintain order.

On July 1, many strikers gathered in Berea and headed to West View over the Big Four Railroad tracks. A group of deputies also headed to West View by way of Olmsted Falls and arrived first. When the strikers got there, a hand-to-hand fight ensued. Then someone, reportedly a striker, fired a shot.

"In the space of a few moments more than fifty shots were exchanged," the *New York Times* reported the next day. "Three of the strikers were seen to fall. Two of them were dragged into the woods by their companions. The name of the man who lies at the quarries wounded is John M. Cholski. He has family in Berea. Immediately after the fight, the strikers fled. They went to Berea in bunches."

In the July 10, 1896, *Berea Advertiser*, a report from West View noted, "Our little burgh has taken on a military aspect; the Rocky River quarry is being guarded by about 30 men from Company K."

The State Board of Arbitration intervened by July 14 and brought both sides together for talks at the company's Berea office on July 25. The board reported that the meeting "was remarkable for the spirit of fairness and good feeling manifested by all parties. As a result of the conference an amicable agreement was entered into, and the strike ended and the military was withdrawn." The board determined the strike cost workers $19,500 in wages, the company $40,000, and the state $10,400 for National Guard services.

As the strike ended, people in and around quarry towns looked forward to conditions returning to normal. But the best days of the Olmsted Falls quarries were past. In December 1896, Cleveland Stone transferred Tom Barnum (son of Luther), eight-year supervisor of the Olmsted Falls quarries, to a larger operation in Grindstone City, Michigan. Tom later returned to Ohio as superintendent of the Berea quarries. Still later, the company promoted him to general superintendent of all Cleveland Stone operations. His brother, Harry, eventually ran the quarry at Peninsula, Ohio.

In November 1897, the *Advertiser* reported about Olmsted Falls:

> *The Cleveland Stone Company's quarries located here are not worked as extensively as usual this season and the hundreds of laborers who formerly found employment in the quarries have found other means of earning a livelihood.*

In May 1898, the newspaper reported that "the Cleveland Stone Co. is intending to put down their men at West View, to three days per week. With $2 per sack for flour and $1 per bushel for potatoes we cannot see how laboring men with large families are to exist." But West View and Columbia Township quarries continued longer than those in Olmsted Falls. In the late 1920s, Cleveland Stone still listed West View as one of its major operations, but quarrying did not continue there much longer. After the first third of the twentieth century, the center of activity for Cleveland Stone and its successor companies shifted to Amherst in Lorain County, where it continued into the twenty-first century.

OIL FEVER—AND THEN GAS

Oil sparked interest beginning in 1875, when the *Advertiser* reported that an unidentified school board member was enticed by such promises as "eighty barrels of oil…pumped from a single well in a day, selling at twenty dollars per barrel, and a chance for all to invest and get rich." Soon, such entrepreneurs as L.C. Tanney in West View and the Osborn Bros. & Rathbun Oil Company in Olmsted Falls set up derricks and began drilling. Osborn & Rathbun began using horsepower but switched to an engine within weeks. By late January 1876, the *Advertiser* reported, "They are down 76 feet, and getting nearer China daily."

In February 1876, A.B. Barnard, E.A. Barnard and W. Daily were reported to be drilling half a mile west of Olmsted Falls. The *Advertiser* also reported, "The oil fever is still raging and some are getting it so bad that a person can almost smell it in their breath." One week later, the paper noted:

> *Oil companies are springing up like mushrooms after a warm shower. Scarcely a week passes but that we hear of the preparations of some parties who intend to drill for oil…Many are watching the results of the different parties and if they succeed the prospects are that the town will boast of a score of oil companies before many days.*

But by spring, oil fever had cooled off. One operation drilled 170 feet without finding oil. "There ain't near as much oil under Olmsted as people supposed," the *Advertiser* reported on April 6, 1876. "Oil stock is cheap, nearly as cheap as Plank Road stock." On June 15, the paper declared, "The oil excitement has died out entirely, leaving quite a number of citizens wiser if not sadder."

Drillers sometimes tapped into natural gas. It was regarded at worst as a nuisance and at best as meager consolation for a few residents to heat and light their homes. But more than a decade later, attitudes changed.

"The citizens of this place are agitating the question of natural gas," a West View correspondent wrote in February 1887. "There are very good indications."

By May 1888, West View had two natural gas wells. More wells were drilled in the 1890s. At Butternut Ridge in 1890, D.K. Huntington was reported to have "gas on the brain," but he struck gas and hoped to have enough to light his house. Later that year, C. DeRooi drilled in Olmsted Falls.

"Gas! Gas! we've got it," the *Advertiser* reported.

> *On Monday of last week Mr. DeRooi struck a large vein of gas, at a depth of less than 800 feet, throwing the drill from the well and blowing up things in general. There is a great deal of speculative talk, but if there is gas in paying quantities underneath this sleepy town it will certainly be developed.*

Some people wanted Olmsted Falls Council to issue bonds for $1,500 to fund well drilling. They even got state legislators to pass a bill permitting it. The village council was against it, but in April 1991, residents elected a new council that agreed to a referendum. However, at the special election the next month, that proposition lost by a margin of nine votes.

By January 1891, at least nine wells were operating in the township, and people kept drilling.

Here and Gone

Drain tile manufacturing became important in West View. In the early 1880s, postmaster and store owner Ephraim Biglow (sometimes spelled "Bigelow") set up a kiln to make drain tile from local clay. Late in 1884, he closed his mercantile business to devote attention to the tile factory. That year, the company's eight-man crew produced 350,000 tiles ranging from two inches to eight inches wide, as well as 250,000 bricks. But by the mid-1890s, it was hard for Biglow to find enough clay locally. In 1897, he bought a tile company in New London, Ohio, where he relocated the E. Biglow & Son operations.

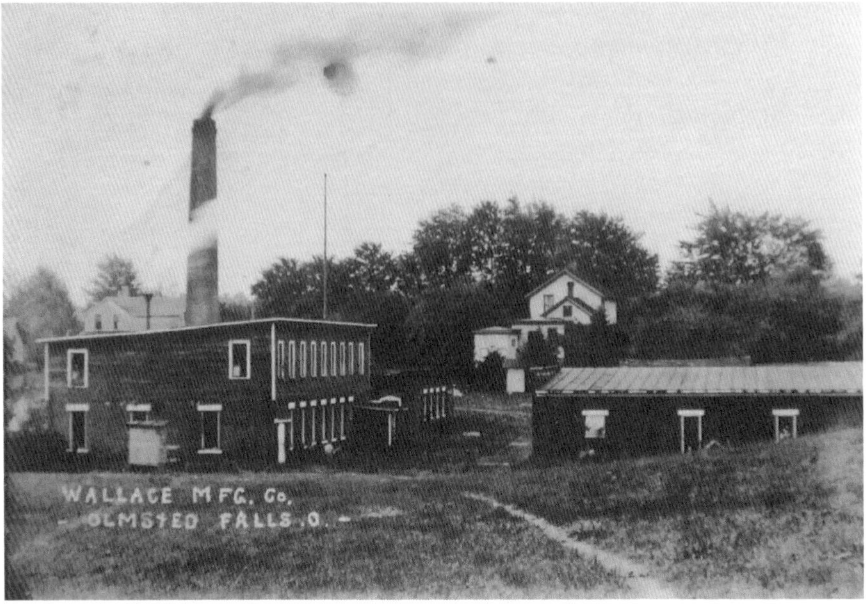

Wallace Manufacturing used the former bending works factory for several years in the early 1900s.

"Mr. and Mrs. E. Biglow and son have left a void here which cannot be easily filled, socially and religiously, and there are a number of men thrown out of employment by the removal of their brick and tile works to New London," the *Advertiser* reported in September 1897. In 1910, an article in a trade journal, *Brick*, made it clear how much West View had lost. It called Biglow "probably the best tile manufacturer on the continent, doing a business which reached 1,000 cars of tile a year. All of his tile are dark red, thin tile, and they are giving the best of satisfaction to both the manufacturer and the patron."

In Olmsted Falls, after Ed Kidney and Gus Leutkemeyer left the bending works in 1901, Wallace Manufacturing Co. later moved into the factory to make lamps, including streetlamps and house lamps. Alright Manufacturing Co. set up nearby to make a range of products, including small stoves and bicycles. Eventually, they merged and employed about fifty people. But the new company lasted only a few more years.

Greenhouses

As small industries moved away or closed, the industry left was again mainly agricultural. That included farms throughout the township and even within the village. Early in the twentieth century, some farmers started using greenhouses to extend the growing season. The area around Olmsted Falls, West View, Olmsted Township, Schaaf Road in Brooklyn Heights, Sheffield and Avon had a large concentration of greenhouses.

As early as 1881, Theodore Schueren operated a nursery and greenhouses near Turkeyfoot Cemetery. In 1887, L.B. Adams, writing in the *Advertiser*, called Schueren's property

> *some of the most beautiful surroundings imaginable. Here plots of geraniums of all varieties, dahlias, tube and monthly roses, all snugly rooted in a thousand or more little pots from which they send out a mingled perfume that intoxicates the olfactories and you loathe to leave the spot. From this we were conducted into the spacious hot houses. Here the richness of tropical foliage greets the eye: at our front looms up the India rubber tree (or caoutchoue) with its large waxen leaves; here are orange and lemon trees surrounded by thousands of rare plants of which Mr. Schueren finds ready sale at his reasonable price. The prickly cactus in full bloom seems here as much at home as if in the sunny Mexican soil. These with many other trees, shrubs and plants make the collection one worth miles of travel to see. Mr. Schueren's large nursery extending back nearly one mile, comprises evergreens, cedar, sycamore, poplar and many other varieties which are transplantable every season to beautify our lawns, make our parks, shady walks and evergreen hedges.*

However, Schueren relocated to Rockport (Rocky River) by the early 1890s.

In 1901, Martin Ruetenik, who lived along Schaaf Road, developed a design that set the standard for commercial greenhouses. His were thirty feet wide with pipe supports and steam heat. The water system included a dam, wind power and storage tanks. With a fleet of Model T trucks, Ruetenik distributed fresh produce as far as Pennsylvania and Indiana. One Cleveland newspaper called him "the celery king."

Many greenhouses, including some in Olmsted, were established in the 1920s. In 1933, a *Plain Dealer* article estimated the value of the Cleveland area's greenhouse industry—called "the largest territory of glass in the country"—at $6.6 million. It described how greenhouses competed with farming in Texas, Mexico and the Gulf states. "In greenhouses, a tour revealed, the growers have the vines primed to maximum growth and fastest ripening," reporter John A. Crawford wrote. "A scrawny cucumber four inches long will be eight or nine Monday and ready for market, visitors were told at the Heinrichs greenhouse in West View, on the Lorain County line."

Gayle Hansen, co-owner of Hansen's Greenhouse in Olmsted Falls, said in 2009 that greenhouses located in Olmsted, because

> *there were the creeks and the rivers for water, and for some odd reason, in this county, the Dutch and the Danish settled here, and that's what they brought from Europe. They all had people following them over here. One reason this general area has a lot of greenhouses is because of* [people] *coming from Europe.*

Hansen, who is of Danish descent, said Olmsted Falls and West View greenhouses grew mostly tomatoes in the 1920s; flowers came later. Operators formed a marketing association for tomatoes in 1929 and later added cucumbers, she said.

Many greenhouses sent their produce to the Greenhouse Vegetables Packing Company on the Cuyahoga County Fairgrounds in Berea to be graded and packed before being sent to markets. The 1933 *Plain Dealer* article said that about forty women could pack twenty-five thousand baskets of tomatoes a day.

"In 1965, the Olmsted Falls district alone had 125 acres under glass structure," Hansen said, adding that the section of Columbia Road between Bagley Road and Sprague Road alone had thirteen greenhouses.

> *The proximity to Cleveland is one reason why a lot of them built here. It was just an area where they thought they could promote their crops and sell them to the Cleveland area with all the terminal markets that were down there. The other reason was because there was a major coal company in Olmsted Falls.*

Not all of Olmsted's greenhouses were along Columbia Road. The Hall family began growing vegetables in a greenhouse along McKenzie Road in the township in 1923. Eventually, the Halls covered about 9.5 acres along McKenzie and Cook Roads under three greenhouses. The biggest one, which covered 4.5 acres, grew tomatoes, while the other two grew flowers. The Hall family had previously established a meat processing and distribution business there.

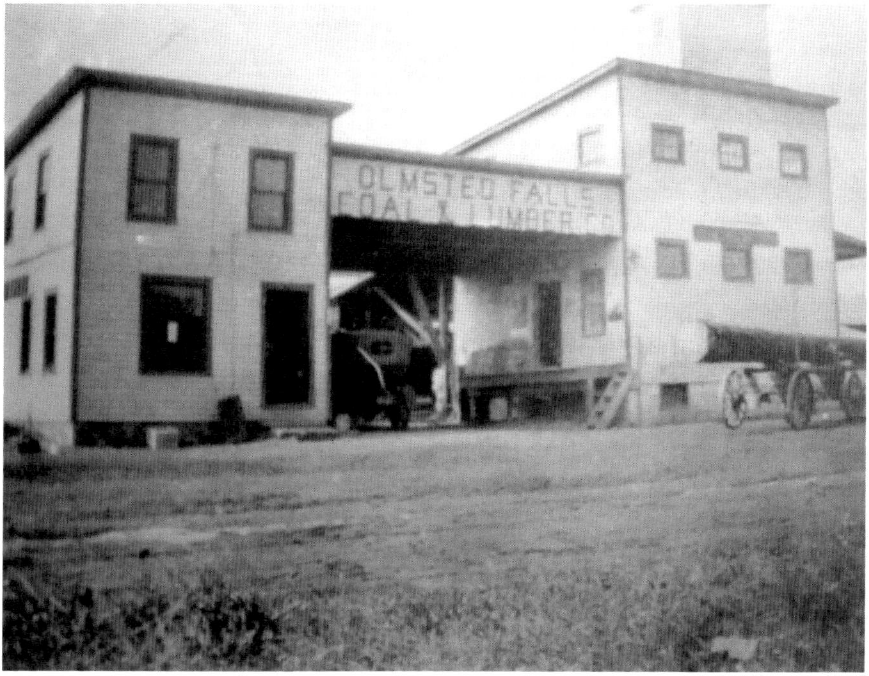

Olmsted Coal & Lumber, which operated north of the railroad tracks and west of Brookside Drive, supplied coal to Olmsted greenhouses.

Most local greenhouses were heated by burning coal in the early years. Railroad lines and spurs that had served the quarries proved useful for getting coal to greenhouses. For example, Schuster's Greenhouse, started in 1924, heated 1.5 acres under glass by the late 1940s with a coal boiler. Many greenhouses later switched to natural gas or oil heat.

In 1972, the *Plain Dealer* reported that the Cleveland area had more than four hundred acres under glass, making it "the largest greenhouse area in the country." But the business was threatened by increased labor costs, rising heating bills and competition from Mexico and California. The article cited Elmo Caruthers, manager of Westview Greenhouse Co., 9191 Columbia Road, as saying his company had to produce 22,000 baskets of tomatoes an acre to turn a profit—up from about 15,000 baskets fifteen years earlier. He said Westview Greenhouse produced 121,000 baskets of tomatoes in 1971. With 5.6 acres under glass, Caruthers said, it cost $10,000 a year to heat each acre.

Operators growing tomatoes were especially hurt because tomatoes from Florida, California and Mexico were about twenty cents a pound cheaper than those from greenhouses. Some greenhouses went out of business. Others switched to lettuce, which could be grown at cooler temperatures, or flowers.

The greenhouses that survived and still grew tomatoes by the late 1980s received another blow. Freezing weather destroyed much of Florida's tomato crop in December 1989. Northern Ohio greenhouses could not take advantage of that opportunity because their tomatoes were not ready for harvest. Florida growers quickly replanted all at once, so instead of having tomatoes ripen at different times, they all ripened simultaneously. When those Florida tomatoes were ripe in March 1990, they glutted the market at prices much lower than greenhouse tomatoes. Some greenhouses did not survive.

"Olmsted Falls is one of the last agricultural areas in the county with the three greenhouses we still have," Hansen said in 2009. "Spots like Schaaf Road still have a couple left, but the big boys are all gone. We're one of the last areas of agriculture."

The greenhouses still operating in Olmsted Falls included: Hansen's Greenhouse, 8781 Columbia Road; Schuster's Westview Gardens, 9164 Columbia Road; and Uncle John's Plant Farm, 8579 Columbia Road. Olmsted Township had Rottel's Greenhouse, 27085 Bagley Road.

VITAMIX

Olmsted Township tried with little success after World War II to attract industry. A notable exception was the Vitamix Corporation, which William G. Barnard founded in 1921. It moved to the township in 1948 to make high-end food blenders.

Barnard sold household products at fairs during the Depression and established a downtown Cleveland health food store, the Natural Foods Institute. In 1937, he introduced the first Vitamix blender. Soon after the advent of television in the late 1940s, Barnard recognized its marketing benefits. In 1949, he bought a half hour on WEWS, Channel 5, for a direct-response commercial, which was broadcast in many markets for several years. Some in the direct-marketing industry have called it the first infomercial.

After years under the name Natural Food, Inc., the company switched to its product name in 1964, becoming Vitamix Corporation. Barnard's son, Bill, and his wife, Ruth, took over the business in 1955. In the 1980s, their son, Grover, became company president with his brother, John, in charge of engineering. They expanded the product line from household blenders to commercial blenders beginning in 1986. John later succeeded Grover as president. In 2009, Jodi (Barnard) Berg assumed the presidency, representing the fourth generation of the Barnard family to run the company.

In 2002, Vitamix began a $3 million expansion project that added sixty-three thousand square feet to its thirty-six-thousand-square-foot plant at 8615 Usher Road. That allowed the company to bring back some production and warehousing operations that had been in Berea. At that time, the company had 145 employees. In 2009, Vitamix had 220 employees and exported its products to more than eighty countries.

DairyPak

In such a residential community as Olmsted Falls, the DairyPak plant stood out ever since it was built in 1957. DairyPak was a subsidiary of Champion Paper and Fiber Company (later Champion International Corporation) when it chose to build a 144,000-square-foot plant at 7920 Mapleway Drive for making gable-top milk cartons. At the time, DairyPak had plants in several states, but its first plant and headquarters were at 5250 Brookpark Road in Cleveland, where about 50 people were employed. The Olmsted Falls plant replaced the Cleveland plant. By 1967, the plant employed 150 people and produced 70 million milk cartons, ranging in size from half a pint to two gallons, each month. They were shipped to dairies in the United States and several foreign countries.

In 1997, Champion International put all of its DairyPak plants and a North Carolina paper mill up for sale but had trouble finding a buyer. In 1999, Champion sold them to about 2,200 employees as part of a $200 million deal. The new employee-owned company was called Blue Ridge Paper Products, Inc. The employee buyout averted possible closure, but employment at the Olmsted Falls plant dropped from more than 200 workers to about 165.

In July 2007, Blue Ridge Paper Products merged with Evergreen Packaging, Inc., and formed the Evergreen Packaging Group, which was then purchased by Rank Group of New Zealand.

North Olmsted

After North Olmsted split from Olmsted Township, its industrial and commercial development diverged from the rest of Olmsted. Beginning in the 1950s with the construction of the Great Northern Shopping Center, North Olmsted became a big commercial center. The city also attracted a number of industries, such as the headquarters of Moen Incorporated, a manufacturer of faucets and related products.

Residents of Olmsted Township and Olmsted Falls benefited from the shopping and employment opportunities available in North Olmsted but had trouble developing their own industrial tax base.

BUILDINGS

HISTORIC AND MOVING

Anyone interested in Olmsted's history is fortunate that scores of buildings significant to the community's past have been preserved and restored. A 1993 survey found about 170 historically significant buildings just within Olmsted Falls. Astonishingly, quite a number of Olmsted's buildings were moved.

For example, in December 2008, a former Baltimore & Ohio Railroad depot traveled about two miles down Columbia Road. That was its second move. It was built in 1895 as a station for Berea (although it was located in Middleburg Heights). In 1969, Gerald Brookins acquired it and moved it to his Trolleyville, USA, in Olmsted Township. In 2008, Clint Williams acquired the depot from Trolleyville, which closed in 2002. To get it to its current location along Mill Street at Grand Pacific Junction, Williams had to cut the top off and have trucks move the building in two pieces so it could pass below utility wires. The move took about three hours.

But several of Olmsted's buildings were moved in the 1800s, long before heavy motorized vehicles. Usually, residents followed a New England tradition called a "drawing bee," in which neighbors contributed enough oxen or horses for a team to move a building on logrollers. An 1883 newspaper article mentioned a drawing bee that used "eleven span of horses" to relocate a house from a low-lying area to a hilltop within a few hours.

HOLY ROLLER

One of the most notable instances of relocating a building occurred in 1873, when the original St. Mary's Catholic Church was moved from the northern end of downtown Olmsted Falls (where the Olmsted Community Church is now) to the southern end near what are now Columbia and Bagley Roads. While the church rolled slowly down the street, Father E.J. Murphy baptized a baby, Rose Sanderson, inside of it.

That building, which was later enlarged, no longer exists. On January 24, 1948, during negative four degrees Fahrenheit weather, the coal furnace overheated and the building burned down. Ground was broken the following September 5 for a brick replacement, which was dedicated on May 20, 1950.

A GRAND MOVE

The biggest building that moved was the Grand Pacific Hotel. It was built as the Rocky River Seminary sometime in the 1830s or the year 1840 along Lewis Road (then Seminary Road). In 1858, the building was moved to its current location (Columbia Road and Mill Street) to become a hotel. That was a long journey for a three-story building, especially going from the east side of the Rocky River to the west side. Some people—including Russell Simmerer, who once owned the building with his brothers—thought that it was moved across the frozen river in the winter. But that would have been very difficult, even if it were moved in pieces, considering the steep banks on both sides. Another possibility is that the movers rolled it across the railroad bridge, which was in place at the time of the move.

In 2006, Williams, who bought the building in 1989 and restored it, shed some light on how that could have been possible. He had discovered that "the whole thing is just like a solid pasteboard box, and it's very, very sturdy." For example, it has big beams that go across the floor and ceiling and up the walls to hold it together in the middle. Gesturing from the front to the back, Williams said, "You could probably pick up this end of it and you'd go back and pick up this end, but this whole thing would just come up." Although he didn't move the Grand Pacific Hotel, Williams had experience moving other buildings at Grand Pacific Junction.

Thomas Brown, the first proprietor of the hotel, called it Grand Pacific Hotel, which both exaggerated its size and seemed misplaced geographically.

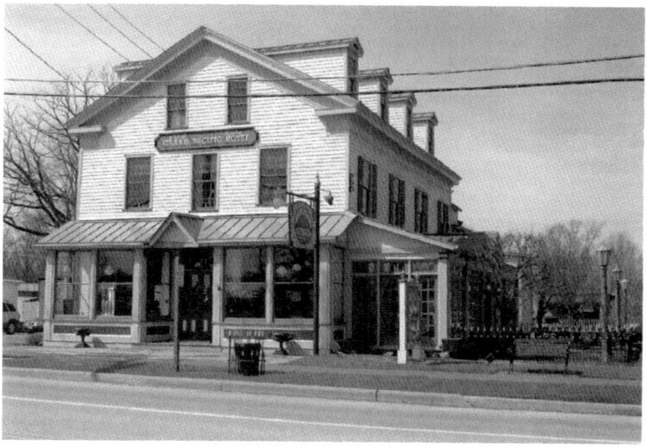

Clint Williams restored the name and much of the early appearance of the Grand Pacific Hotel after it spent more than a century as first a hardware store and then a furniture store annex. *Photo by Jim Wallace.*

The hotel changed hands in the years after Brown's disappearance in an apparent robbery-murder while he traveled to Cleveland. Nicholas Moley was listed as proprietor in 1872, but Loren Fitch was listed as manager in 1874. However, W.S. Carpenter soon acquired it and renamed it Hotel DeCarpenter. Although it was advertised as being "elegant," it housed many transients in the years 1874 and 1875, according to a newspaper report. That was because township trustees offered any transient a free meal and a free night of lodging, a policy that was later dropped. In 1877, the building became the Dougherty Hotel after Frank Dougherty bought it for $2,000.

In 1893, Joe Peltz and Philip Simmerer, brothers-in-law, bought the building for use as a hardware and drugstore. That turned out to be the longest use of the building, first as Peltz & Simmerer Hardware and then as Simmerer & Sons Hardware. While the first floor was chock-full of goods for home and farm, second-floor space was rented to a doctor and a dentist. The old third-floor ballroom was used to manufacture corn planters and other hand tools.

Peltz left the hardware business in 1912 and returned to running a drugstore. Simmerer went on for several decades longer, bringing three of his four sons—Clarence, Oscar and Russell—into the business. The sons finally closed the hardware in September 1971. The building then became Kucklick's Village Square Shoppe Annex, a storage building for furniture sold at Kucklick's store in the Depositors Bank Building.

In 1989, Williams bought it and other buildings nearby. He restored the name Grand Pacific Hotel and the buildings to create Grand Pacific Junction.

Jail Tales

Another Grand Pacific Junction building that is not where it started is the old jail, built about 1860. For many years, it stood on what is now the Olmsted Community Church parking lot. Made of wood twelve feet by fourteen feet, the jail had a window with iron bars and a thick wooden door.

Sometime in the 1800s, the town marshal reportedly arrested the mayor for a disturbance at a saloon and put him in jail. After the mayor got out, he fired the marshal and appointed a replacement. The mayor returned to drunken celebration, and the new marshal put him back in jail.

In 1924, the village moved the jail to Mill Street west of the Simmerers' store to house the village's new Model T fire truck.

After Williams began developing Grand Pacific Junction, he moved the old jail closer to Grand Pacific Hotel. He also cut the back off the little building. "So I added eight feet to it, and that gave me enough for a bathroom," he said. Since then, it has been known as the Olde Jail House and has housed such merchants as an ice cream shop and, later, a honey shop.

Other Junction Moves

The Carriage House at Grand Pacific Junction was built around 1860. It was associated with a house destroyed in a fire on January 8, 1913. Also

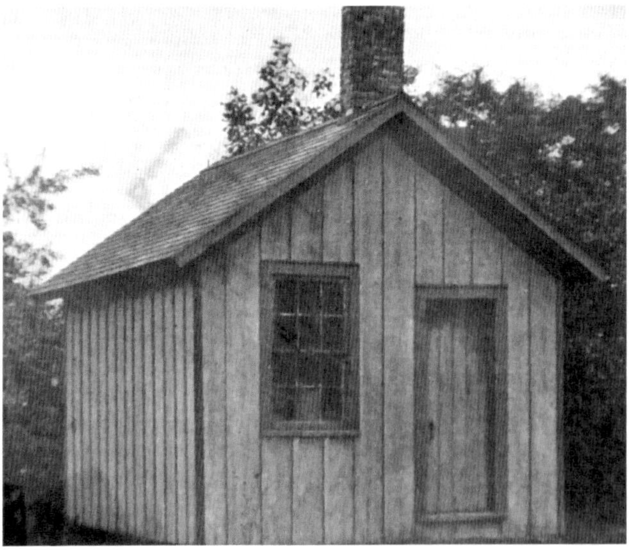

The jail was smaller before its renovation to become a Grand Pacific Junction shop.

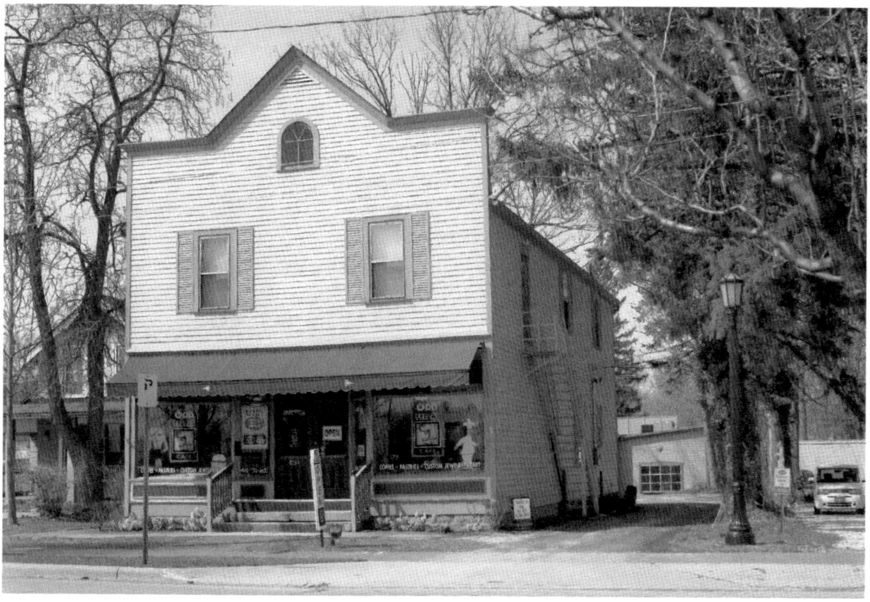

The former Odd Fellows Hall sits a block and a half south and on the other side of the street from where it was built. *Photo by Jim Wallace.*

destroyed were a store and a tin shop where the Depositor's Bank Building now stands. Later, the Carriage House was moved behind that building to become storage space for Kucklick's Village Square Shoppe. Williams moved it to its current location near the former stables building and restored it for use as a gift shop.

The building at 8154 Columbia Road, known as the Grange Hall, took on the name Odd Fellas Café in the twenty-first century for good reason. It was built in 1905 as the second Odd Fellows Hall. The first one stood just north of the railroad tracks on the east side of Columbia Road (now the parking lot of Falls Veterinary Clinic, 8017 Columbia Road). It burned down on August 3, 1903, from sparks from a passing railroad engine. The building housed the meeting place for the Independent Order of Odd Fellows and merchants, such as Art Dodd's grocery store.

The Odd Fellows built their new hall at the same site. But in 1909, the railroad widened its bridge to accommodate more tracks, so the Odd Fellows moved the building to its current location, 8154 Columbia Road. After Odd Fellows membership dropped, the Olmsted Grange, which promoted agricultural interests, occupied the building until 2003. The building is now part of Grand Pacific Junction.

Moving into New Roles

The building housing the Olmsted Falls Branch of the Cuyahoga County Public Library moved twice. Newton Loomis built it for his home after he moved to Olmsted in 1834. Originally, it stood at what is now the site of the Falls Veterinary Clinic. St. Mary's used it as a parish house from 1858 to 1873. Early in the twentieth century, the Olmsted Community Church acquired the house and moved it to where the church's parking lot now stands. In 1955, the church donated the house for use as a library, and it was moved across Main Street. About $1,000 was spent furnishing it. The library added a new wing in 1965 and renovated the building in 1989.

The Olmsted Falls Depot also sits in a different place than where the Lake Shore & Michigan Southern Railroad built it. When opened in 1876, it was located near Division Street (now Mapleway Drive). Berea's *Grindstone City Advertiser* said the depot was 108 feet long and 30 feet wide. The paper also said:

> *It contains ladie's* [sic] *sitting room, gentlemen's sitting room, ticket office, telegraph office, and baggage room. The building is finished in fine style, and is an ornament to the village and a credit to the Railroad Company.*

But Olmsted residents thought it was too far from the center of town. In 1900, it was put on rollers and hauled by a locomotive to the other end of South Depot Street (now Garfield Street) near Brookside Drive.

The depot had passenger rail service until 1948 and freight delivery until 1954. The railroad, then the New York Central, used the depot for storage and as a maintenance-of-way facility until about 1965. It later was used for restoring and selling antiques. A fire burned the depot in 1972, but the fire department was across the street on Brookside Drive, so the fire was extinguished quickly. After the depot was vacant for several years, members of the Cuyahoga Valley & West Shore Model Railroad Club leased it from then-owner Conrail beginning in 1977 and restored it for use as a meeting place and to display members' model railroad collections. The club bought the building in 1996.

On November 9, 1988, something else moved in next door to the depot: a rusty, 56,800-pound, 1951 Pennsylvania Railroad caboose. Conrail donated it to the model railroad club, which cleaned, repaired and painted it for permanent display.

Northern Movers

Several other old buildings from the section of township that became North Olmsted were moved to preserve them at the Olmsted Historical Society's Frostville Museum at the corner of Lewis and Cedar Point Roads in the Cleveland Metroparks' Rocky River Reservation. They include:

The Briggs House (1836): Built by carpenter John Ames for Thomas and Abiah Briggs and their six children, who had moved to Olmsted from Vermont in 1817. It was located at what is now the north side of Lorain Road west of Stearns Road.

The Carpenter House (1830): John and Lucina Carpenter built this house along the current Lorain Road about two years after they moved to Olmsted from Vermont.

Jenkins's Cabin (1820 or earlier): Benjamin Clark built this cabin for his family of eight. It was on the east side of Columbia Road just south of the current North Olmsted–Westlake border. But Clark did not own the land. The owner, Asher M. Coe, evicted Clark in 1823 after Coe arrived from Connecticut. Eventually, William Jenkins and then Joseph Jenkins, apparently his brother, occupied the cabin.

Barton Road Church (1847): Originally called the Methodist Episcopal Church of Butternut Ridge, it was located at what is now the corner of Lorain and Barton Roads.

The Prechtel House (1876): Became the home of Martin and Margaret Prechtel, German immigrants, shortly after Adam Poe built it. It is the only house that originally stood at the site of the Frostville Museum. Also on the museum grounds are two barns and a general store.

Stationary but Changing

Olmsted Falls has several other buildings from the 1800s and early 1900s that have never moved. Most of those in commercial use have become part of Grand Pacific Junction. One of the oldest is the Grand Pacific Wedding Chapel at 7970 Columbia Road, which was built in 1853 as a Methodist Episcopal church for $1,555. In 1889, the Methodists remodeled it. The church was directly across the street from the Congregational church. Over the years, the two churches sometimes shared services and Sunday school classes. In 1917, they agreed to merge, forming the Olmsted Community

Church with the Methodist building used for services and the Congregational building used for Sunday school and community activities. In the 1950s, the current Olmsted Community Church was built. The Christian education wing was dedicated on February 26, 1956, and the sanctuary was dedicated on March 20, 1960. The former Congregational church was torn down to make room for the current church parking lot. In 1956, the Olmsted Falls Masonic Lodge bought the former Methodist church for $25,000. In 2001, Williams bought it, restored it and made it a nondenominational wedding chapel. The restoration included rebuilding the bell tower and steeple that had been blown off during a 1910 storm.

Almost as old is one of the smallest of Grand Pacific Junction's stores, nicknamed the Doll House. It was built about 1860, at the corner of Orchard and Mill Streets. The house was built with only four rooms plus a basement with quarry-stone walls and a dirt floor. The house lacked central heating or plumbing until 1943.

Despite its size, the house was originally the home of immigrant William TeGrotenhuis, whose name means "the big house" in Dutch. He made wooden shoes in a factory behind the house, as well as some trouble for himself. At least twice, he was sued for having relations with women not married to him. The second time, in 1880, when he was sued by the husband of Lena TeLuida, another immigrant, the *Advertiser* reported that "the depreciation placed upon chastity would cause a moralist to weep."

Another very old building, built about 1860, at 7990–7994 Columbia Road once housed a saloon and pool hall. Although he was not the first to run the saloon, Dutch immigrant Herman Fenderbosch was most associated with it after he bought the building for $1,000 in 1887. He ran the saloon until 1904, when his son, Henry, took over. In 1908, the village voted to close all saloons, so Henry went into the grocery business with his brother-in-law, Arthur Dodd, a few doors down. After 1945, Andrew Froehlich operated a shoe repair shop on what had been the saloon side of the building, the northern end. Froelich's son, Walter, operated a dry cleaning store on the pool hall side. That use continued into the twenty-first century as Master Cleaners. Appropriately, the former saloon became the Olde Wine Cellar.

The building that served as the Dodd-Fenderbosch grocery store at 8820–8822 Columbia Road would have been about as old as the former saloon, but much of it was destroyed by a fire on January 19, 1949. The part that was not destroyed was moved to Mapleway Drive to be used as a home. The current building at the Columbia Road site is the replacement built after the fire.

At the Junction

Several Grand Pacific Junction buildings date back to the end of the nineteenth century. Among them are two grand Victorian houses just north of the Grand Pacific Hotel. Joseph Peltz built his house in 1889, when he still operated a drugstore across the street. Philip Simmerer built his house, between Peltz's house and the former hotel, in 1894, one year after he and Peltz converted the hotel into their hardware and drugstore. Both Simmerer and Peltz built additions onto their homes in 1898. The Peltz House escaped destruction in the fire of January 8, 1913, only because Olmsted residents formed a bucket brigade after the fire department's pumper truck ran out of water. Both houses had become run-down before their restoration as part of Grand Pacific Junction. Since then, they have served as retail shops.

Some sources erroneously place the construction of the stable associated with the hotel/hardware store in 1898. The exact date of its construction is uncertain, but it is likely much older than that because the hotel would have needed a place to board the horses of its guests and the hotel quit being a hotel in 1893. Also, in late October 1898, when the *Advertiser* noted that Peltz and Simmerer had built additions to their residences, the correspondent made reference to "that old barn" on the property. In the 1990s, Williams refurbished the stable to be a store and later Clementine's restaurant. Its broad beams, doors and hardware still reflect its original purpose for housing horses.

Two side-by-side Grand Pacific Junction buildings were constructed in 1900. One is known as the Warehouse because it was used as a warehouse for the hardware store. Grand Pacific Junction literature refers to it as "a good example of the flat storefront architecture that was popular around the turn of the century."

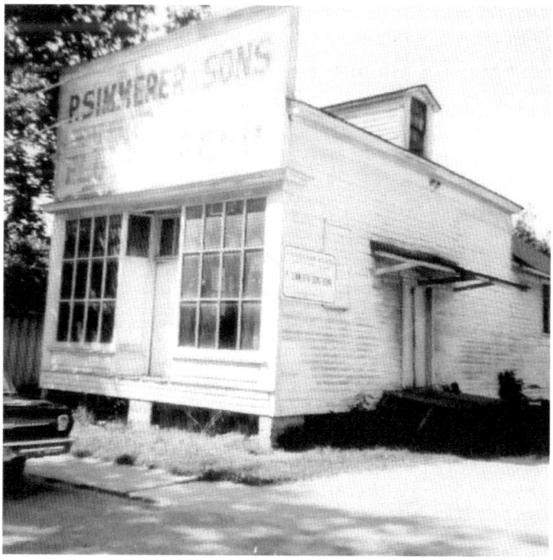

The Granary, which has post-and-beam construction, became one of Grand Pacific Junction's gift shops.

The other 1900 building, known as the Granary, was used as a store for grain, flour and feed. Grand Pacific Junction literature notes, "The original grain bins are still intact on the second floor. Hay was also stored above drop-through trap doors to the first floor loading platforms for the convenience of horse and buggy customers."

The Depositors Bank Building, which occupies the most space at Grand Pacific Junction, was built in 1924 by the Olmsted Dover Saving and Loan Company, which had been formed one year earlier. It was reorganized later as the Depositors Saving and Loan Company. Unfortunately for that company, the prosperous 1920s gave way to the Great Depression of the 1930s. Depositors closed in 1932. After that, a business involved in heating and tinning moved in. In 1940, the building became the home of the Kucklick family's furniture and appliance store. Kucklick's Village Square Shoppe specialized in early American–style furniture and operated for almost fifty years. National City Bank also occupied the north end of the building for many years. After Williams bought the building, he made big changes to open several new storefronts along the long end of its L shape, the side that extends 160 feet back from Columbia Road. He put a wooden boardwalk in front of those stores.

A later addition to Grand Pacific Junction is the stone building at 7989 Columbia Road. It was built from 1940 to 1942 with help from the Works Progress Administration to serve as the Olmsted Falls Town Hall, replacing a wood-frame facility that had been built on the same site in 1883. After Olmsted Falls and West View merged in 1971, the combined municipality had two town halls, so one was designated the North Hall and the other the South Hall. In 1983, the North Hall was renamed the Bonsey Building after Charles Bonsey, the mayor when it was built. In 2001, the city moved its offices out of the building and into the former 1916 school building at the corner of Bagley Road and Mapleway Drive. Years later, Williams renovated the Bonsey Building. In 2008, most of the building became a restaurant called the Moosehead Hoof and Ladder No. 3, with a fire department theme.

THE OLD HOMESTEAD

Not formally a part of Grand Pacific Junction is the yellow house with green trim known as the William Waring Homestead at 8134 Columbia Road. Built as a residence around 1830, it was acquired by Sylvester Alcott in 1874 and James Burns in 1909. It was converted to commercial use later in the

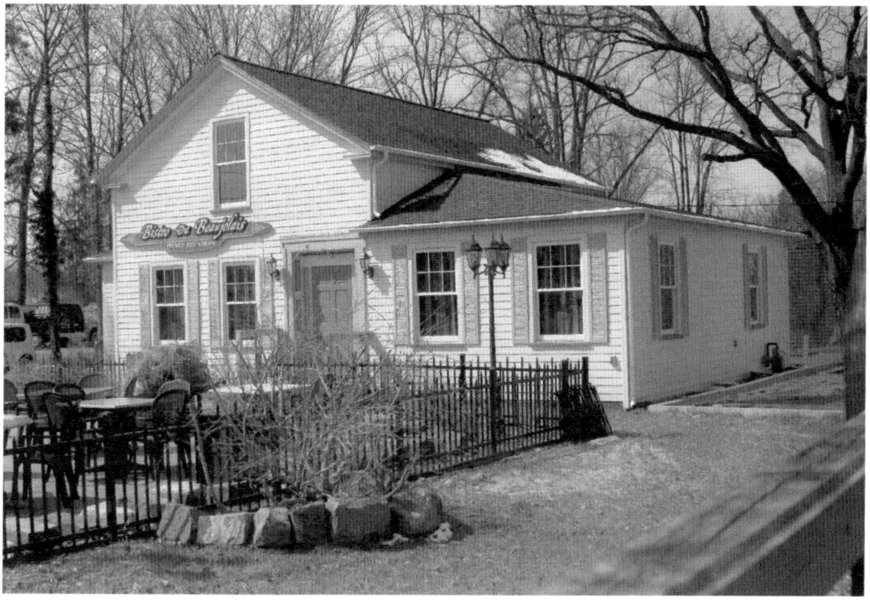

The Waring Homestead is one of the oldest buildings in Olmsted Falls. *Photo by Jim Wallace.*

twentieth century. In 2005, Georges and Claudie d'Arras, natives of France, opened their French restaurant, Le Bistro du Beaujolais, in the building. On the snowy morning of January 10, 2009, a fire caused about $350,000 damage to the building, but the d'Arrases reopened the restaurant with a renovated interior in October of that year. An old icehouse made out of stone is still on the grounds.

Standing Stones

At the southeastern corner of Mill and Orchard Streets is a stone building constructed in 1854 by Waring to be a livery stable and blacksmith shop. It continued to be used as a stable after Burns purchased the Waring House in 1909. In the mid-1900s, Dale and Dorothy Hecker remodeled it into a residence.

One other structure of note in the center of Olmsted Falls remains only partially standing along the west bank of the Rocky River behind Mill River Plaza. It consists of the stone walls that once served as the foundation of Damp's Mill. About 1870, Colonel H.N. Whitbeck built the first mill at the

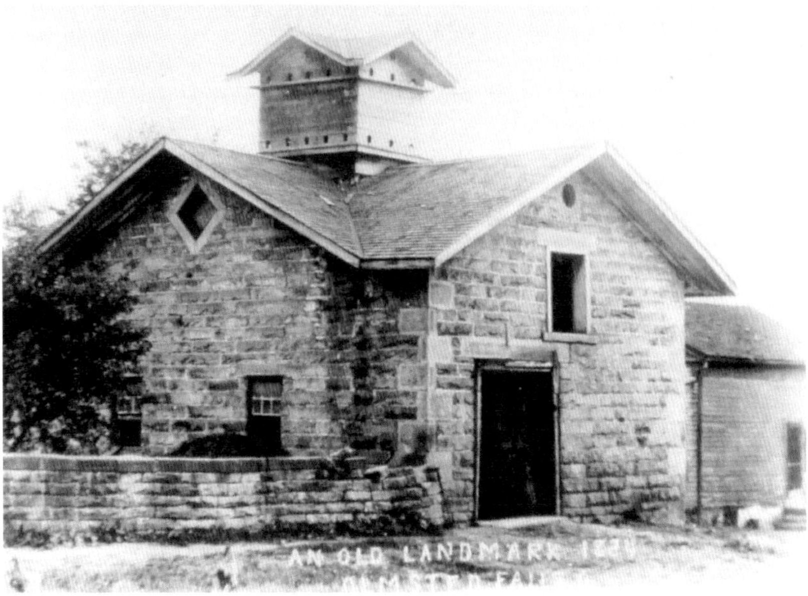

The old stone stable at Mill and Orchard Streets became a residence.

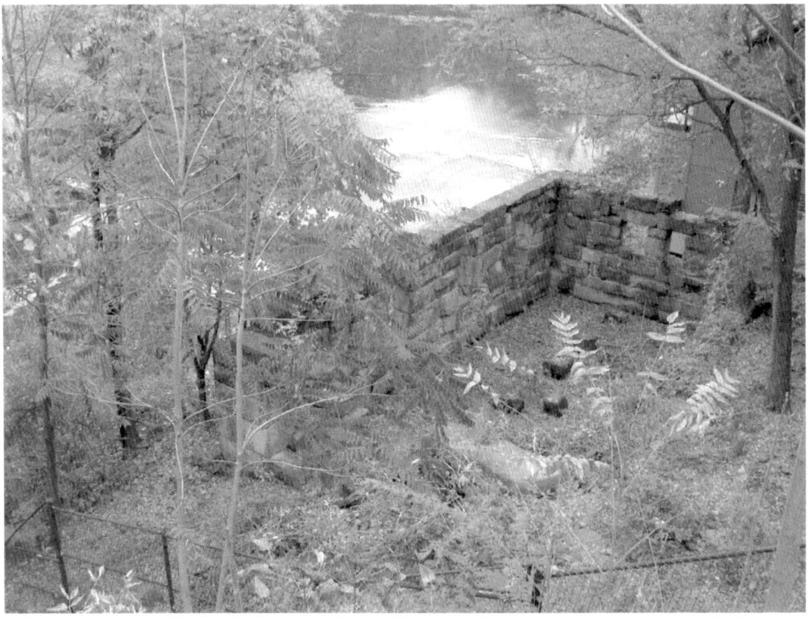

The foundation of Damp's Mill can be viewed from an observation platform near Mill River Plaza. When the river is especially low, an observer can see the curved base of the dam that once held back water for the mill. Large stones from that dam remain along the sides of the river. *Photo by Bruce Banks.*

location. He sold it to Ed Damp in 1876. A flood in March 1883 damaged the mill and its foundation badly. Damp rebuilt it with a thirteen-foot-high foundation in the same spot. In 1906, he sold the mill. Another big flood on March 28, 1913, ruined most of the mill. Later, Stan Capell tore down the wooden structure above the stone foundation and reused some of the parts. The basement door and steps in the home that he and his wife, Millie, shared at 8293 Metropolitan Boulevard came from the mill.

West View, Too

Although the central section of Olmsted Falls contains the highest concentration of old buildings, a few are in the section that was West View. One is the former Wesleyan Methodist Church at the corner of Columbia and Sprague Roads. It was built around 1845 with hand-hewn timber. This building also was moved to be closer to the corner in 1887, facing what is now Columbia Road. The congregation quit using the building in 1974 after constructing a new church in Columbia Township. The building came close to being torn down in 1983 after its condition had declined, but its destruction was averted. In 1988, there was a plan to move the building to the Olmsted Historical Society's Frostville Museum, but that did not happen.

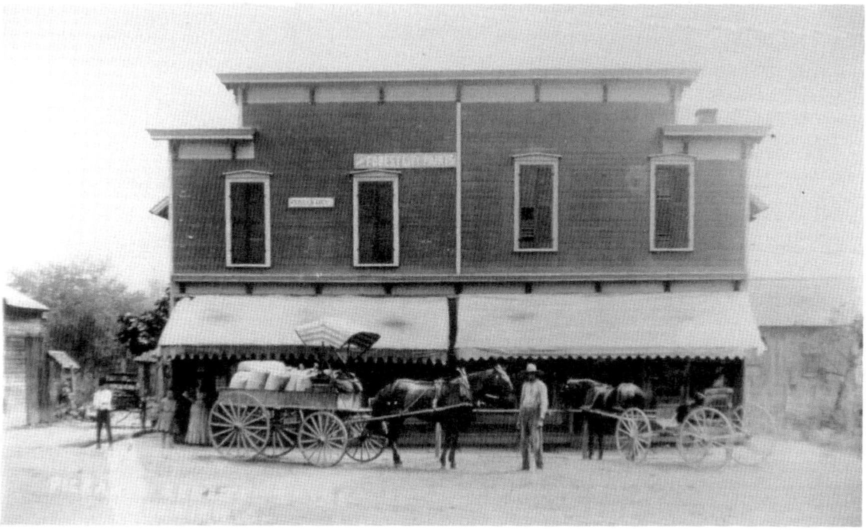

This Italianate-style building, built in West View in the 1870s, remains in use.

North of the old church and just south of the railroad tracks along the east side of Columbia Road stand two buildings that remain from West View's small nineteenth-century business district.

The former West View Town Hall, which was built in 1880 as a two-story schoolhouse, stands on the west side of Columbia Road. The building was renovated into a one-story structure in the twentieth century.

Century-Plus Homes

Throughout Olmsted Falls and Olmsted Township, many houses date back to the 1800s. Like other historic buildings, most of them are in central Olmsted Falls, especially along River Road, Water Street and Columbia Road. Several are marked by signs noting their status as Century Homes, but others are not. The following are some of them, with their years of construction (some disputed) and the owners for whom they are best known:

Dryden-Knowlton House (1835), 7993 Lewis Road: Captain C.P. Dryden and Harriet Howe Dryden bought land here in 1834 and built the house on it. One of their daughters, Hannah, married Dr. A.P. Knowlton, a physician who had served in the Union Army Medical Corps, on January 16, 1869. In 1870, they bought the Dryden home on what was then called Seminary Road.

Eli and Sabra Fitch House (1834), 8566 Lewis Road: Eli was one of six Fitch brothers who moved to Olmsted from East Windsor, Connecticut, in 1831. He married Sabra Cady in 1827. They had ten children.

Philo Bradford House (1851 or earlier), 7435 River Road: Philo Bradford, born in Vermont in 1807, came to Olmsted with his family in 1820. In 1834, he married twenty-one-year-old Delight Underhill. They bought the land here from Eliphalet Williams of Massachusetts, who had acquired it in 1819, following the death of Daniel Phoenix. Phoenix had bought it from the Connecticut Land Company. In the mid-twentieth century, owners Wilbur and Helen Staten added a living room.

Freeman Bradford House (1870), 7542 River Road: Freeman was a son of Lester Bradford, who had operated an inn at the junction of Nobottom and Bradford (now River) Roads. Lester and his brother, Eastman, also operated a brick factory nearby. Freeman ran a dairy farm until he moved to Cleveland in 1888 to go into the grocery business.

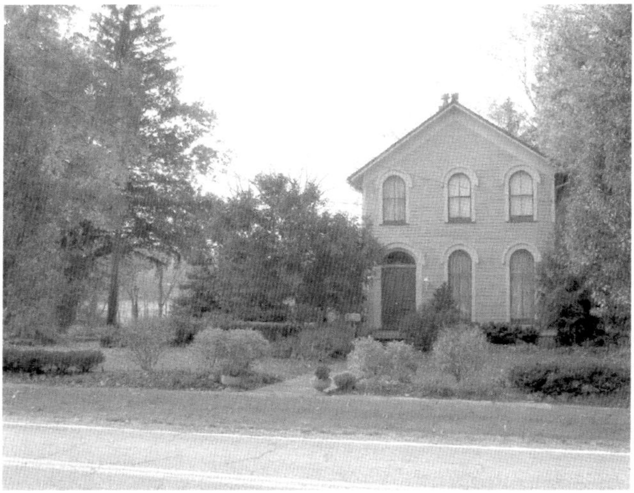

Inventor and entrepreneur Ed Kidney lived in this house at 7562 River Road.

Asher M. Coe House (1840), 7557 River Road: The Coe name is associated more with the Coe Ridge (Lorain Road) area of North Olmsted, which was part of Dover Township when Asher and Abigail Coe moved there in 1823. But this was one of several properties Coe owned in Olmsted Township.

Edward Kidney House (1860), 7562 River Road: Ed Kidney, born in 1847, served in a Civil War artillery unit. He operated a bending works, which made wagon and buggy parts near the house.

John Neumann House (1854), 7569 River Road: A large fireplace in the house was made from Rocky River stones.

Peter Kidney House (1835), 7601 River Road: Peter Kidney, father of Ed Kidney, was born in 1804 in New York and came with his wife, Asenath, to Olmsted in 1833. He initially built a log cabin but replaced it with this larger house. He built a sawmill and a gristmill and made tools, cheese boxes and wooden buckets. His house was initially very primitive, but Kidney added on to it over about twenty years.

Lemuel Hoadley House (1836), 7707 Main Street: Hoadley built his house with help from his son-in-law, John Barnum, to be near their mill along Plum Creek near the Rocky River. The house also is associated with Dr. William Mahoney, a physician who served as a councilman and mayor of Olmsted Falls in the 1960s and 1970s.

Sanford and Clarissa Fitch House (1837), 25347 Water Street: Sanford was one of six Fitch brothers who came to Olmsted in 1831. Sanford and Clarissa moved to Wadsworth, Ohio, in 1847.

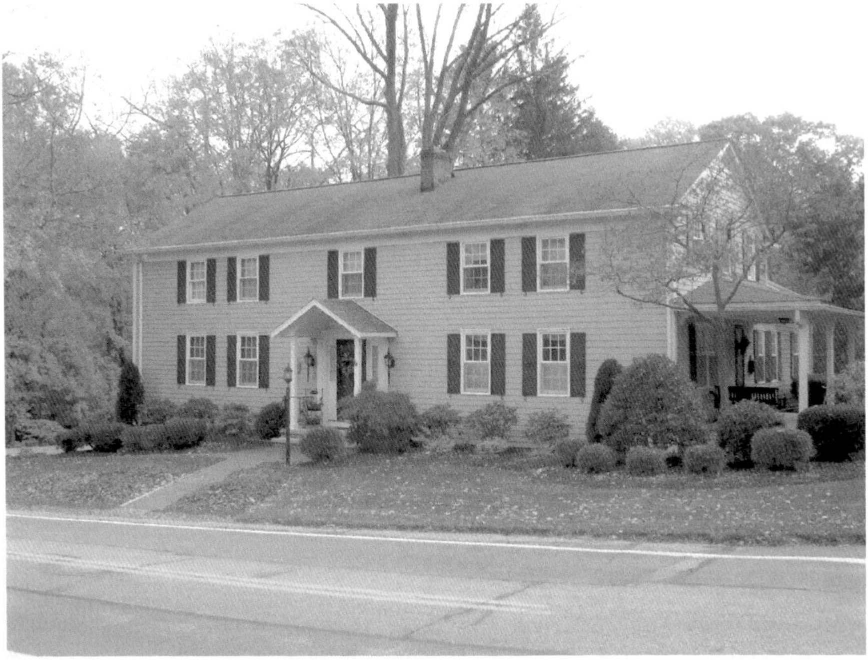

Former mayor William Mahoney lived in this house, built by Lemuel Hoadley, until his death in 1991. The Village Green gazebo was named for Mahoney. *Photo by Bruce Banks.*

JOHN AND EUNICE BARNUM HOUSE (1830), 25334 Water Street: In 1820, John Barnum bought a large tract that ran from the present Village Green to part of the current property of the Olmsted Community Church. He built this house in 1830. It was expanded in 1880. Barnum worked with Lemuel Hoadley on gristmills and sawmills and married Hoadley's daughter, Eunice. They donated land (now Village Green) for a schoolhouse. The house also once served as an inn.

JOHN ADAMS SR. HOUSE (1820), 7315 Columbia Road: This started as a small house, but additions made it one of the largest in Olmsted. Appropriately, in the twentieth century, it became the home of the TeGrotenhuis family, whose name, in Dutch, means "the big house."

SAMUEL LAY JR. HOUSE (1845), 7622 Columbia Road: This is one of the best examples of Greek Revival architecture in Olmsted Falls. It had several additions.

JOHN LAY HOUSE (before 1860), 7642 Columbia Road: John Lay and his brothers, Joseph and Samuel, came to Olmsted Falls in 1855. John and Joseph started a factory that made wooden farm implements and cheese boxes.

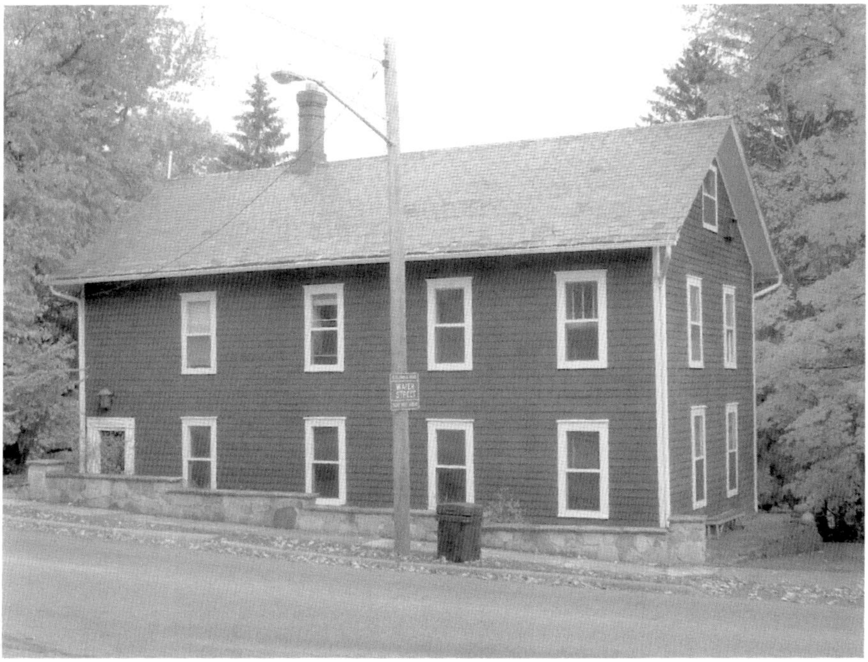

The GAR Hall at 7835 Columbia Road was renovated to become a residence in the twentieth century. *Photo by Bruce Banks.*

Chauncey Mead House (1830), 7674 Columbia Road: Mead, who once served as mayor, built this Western Reserve–style house with tongue-and groove oak flooring and a knotty pine living room ceiling. He and his son operated a harness shop just south of this house. The shop later was replaced by a gas station (Schady's Shell), which Clint Williams renovated to serve as an office for his real estate company.

GAR Hall (1887), 7835 Columbia Road: Thomas Stokes put up this two-story building in the Vernacular style for storage of lumber and other materials from his sawmill. He let the veterans' group, Grand Army of the Republic, use the second story for meetings, which is why it was called the GAR Hall.

Charles and Julia Carter Northrop House (1842), 7872 Columbia Road: This is one of many Greek Revival–style buildings in Olmsted. The Northrops were a prominent family.

Andrew Peters House (1878), 8007 Columbia Road: This is another example of a building that was moved, but in this case, it was merely turned ninety degrees on the same lot. Peters made and sold shoes here.

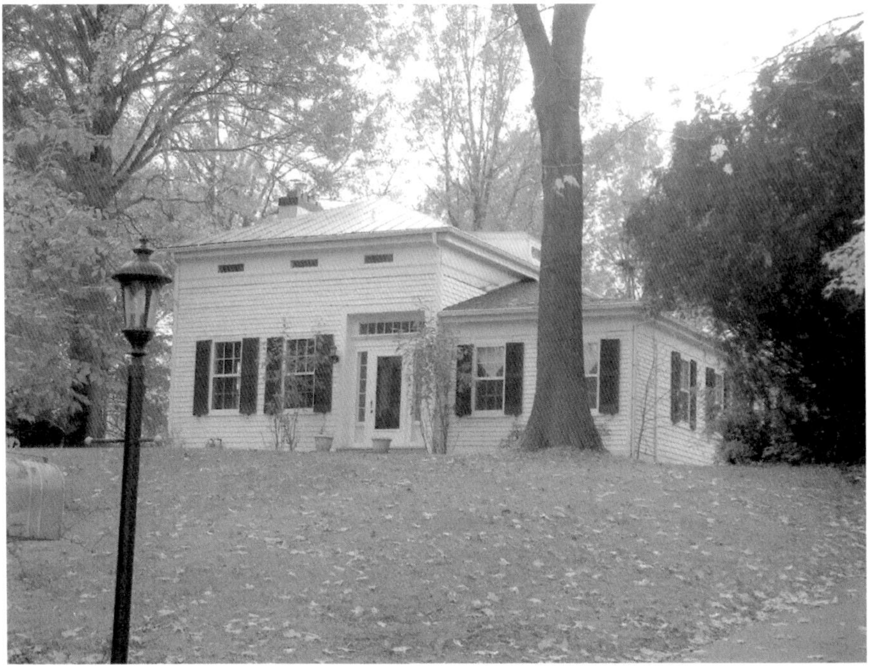

The Northrop House at 7872 Columbia Road once was surrounded by a large estate. *Photo by Bruce Banks.*

HERMAN FENDERBOSCH HOUSE (1853), 8008 Columbia Road: Made of red bricks from Bradford Brick Factory. Leslie A. Harmon has been credited with building this house, but it is best associated with Herman Fenderbosch, who bought it in 1902. It later became the home of his son, Henry.

Another building from the 1800s of note is the barn of John Hall, which stands near the entrance to the Renaissance on John Road. Hall's house—described in 1898 as an "elegant country home"—stood next to it until late in the twentieth century. It served as the clubhouse for Homelinks Golf Course. When the Renaissance was built and the golf course was reconfigured and renamed the Links in the 1980s, the house was removed.

SCHOOLS

In education, Olmsted was a leader—although not right away.

After the first settlers moved into the township, it took several years for schools to be built. That was typical among early Western Reserve communities, where children initially received lessons in small classes held in people's log houses.

Walter Holzworth's and Bernice Offenberg's histories of Olmsted, both written in the 1960s, disagree on where the township's first schoolhouse was built. Offenberg said it was a log house erected in 1821 in the northeastern corner of the township (now the corner of Columbia and Cedar Point Roads). Holzworth said the first one was in the southeastern corner of the township on Calvin Geer's farm. Offenberg also mentioned that building in her account of the early schools.

They also disagree on the location of Olmsted's first frame school building. According to Holzworth, it was built in 1830 on land donated by the Barnum family on what is now the Village Green in Olmsted Falls. Offenberg called that the second frame schoolhouse. She considered a River Road building near Nobottom Road to be the first one. She believed that this location was chosen because Olmsted's only bridge over the Rocky River at that time was on Nobottom Road, so "children across the river would not have to walk so far."

In the mid-1800s, several one-room schools were established. The idea was for students not to have to walk much more than about two miles to school. What developed was a series of subdistricts, each with its own school. Olmsted Township had eight such districts with schools on Kennedy Ridge,

Butternut Ridge, Cook Road, Spafford Road near Barrett Road, Lorain Road near Barton Road, West View, Dutch (Bagley) Road and Sharp Road.

UNION SCHOOL

By 1870, Olmsted Falls residents wanted something better than one-room schools. "Good scholars are a thing of no little importance in any community, but the most successful teachers cannot make them first-class while the buildings they occupy are inconvenient, uncomfortable and dilapidated," a *Grindstone City Advertiser* correspondent wrote. "Nothing is more needed, or will add more largely to the value of property or the quality of our schools in Olmsted village."

Work began in May 1873 on a two-story brick schoolhouse to replace the frame schoolhouse that stood on what became the Village Green. Work progressed slowly. The first classes were held in February 1874 in the Union School. The school was finished that June. The total cost was $9,610.28.

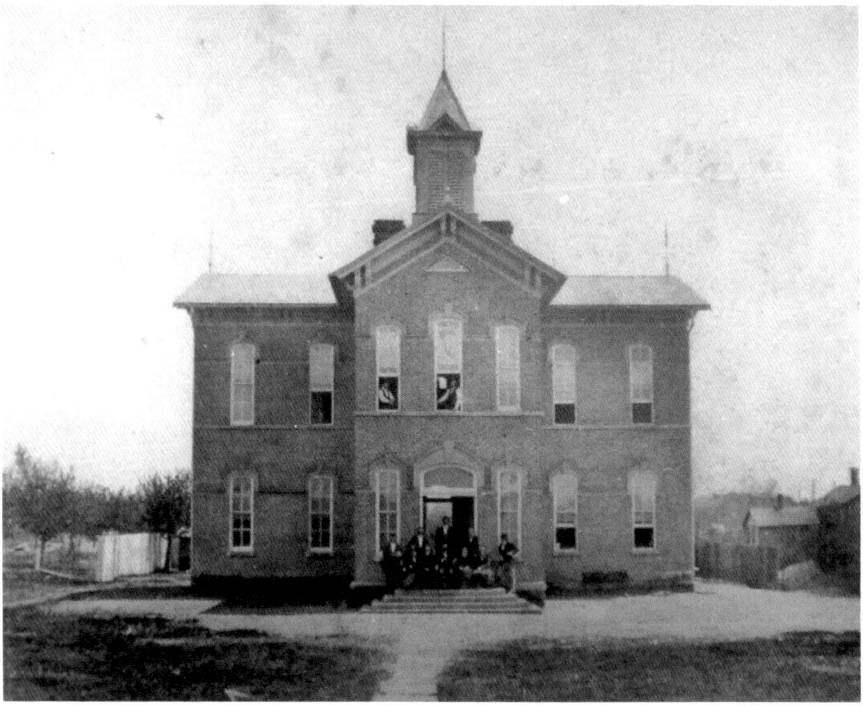

The Union School acquired the nickname the "Big Little Red Schoolhouse."

The school had three departments: primary, intermediate and high school. In early years, it offered only two years of high school. Later, a third year was added, but never the fourth year, so students did not meet qualifications for college enrollment unless they finished high school elsewhere.

In a 1960 essay in Offenberg's book, Loretta Dodd Nickels described the Union School the following way:

> *Entering the door to the left was the first, second and third grades, while the room on the right held the fourth, fifth, and sixth grades. Then there was the big step when the stairs were climbed for the seventh and eighth grades, and in later years the three years of high school.*

Charles Bonsey, who was educated in the building from 1899 to 1911, recalled in 1982, "In my school days, we had one teacher for the first three grades, one teacher for the next three grades and one teacher for the remaining grades—until later, they had to get another teacher." But the district schools scattered around the township had only six grades, he said.

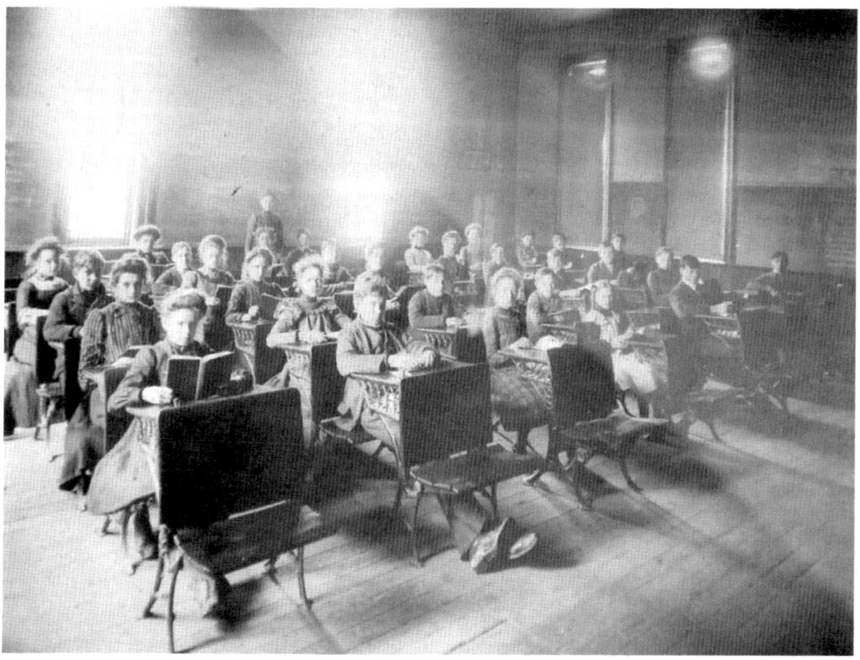

The Union School was considered spacious in the 1800s.

Township Schools

Lura Weitzel, whose mother was a Stearns and whose father was a Hall, attended the District #3 school on the south side of Cook Road, a few lots east of Stearns Road. In 1983, she recalled that it was a one-room school with a girls' outhouse at one corner of the lot and a boys' outhouse at the opposite corner.

In 1889, West View followed the lead of Olmsted Falls and rebuilt its school as a two-story brick structure. (That building later became the town hall after West View incorporated as a village.)

Students from Olmsted Township could attend high schools in neighboring communities with tuition paid by the township. Some students from the central and southern sections of the township rode the Lake Shore and Michigan Southern Railroad to Berea High School. After the streetcar line began along Butternut Ridge in 1895, students from that area could ride it to attend high school in Cleveland and Elyria. Some West View students commuted to high school in Berea, while other students boarded in rooms in Berea during the school year.

Consolidation

Early in the twentieth century, the public education system changed significantly. In 1904, a consolidated, five-member board of education was formed for the township with jurisdiction over all the rural subdistricts. The board appointed a superintendent for the entire district and directors for each subdistrict.

After North Olmsted became a village in 1909, the schools within its limits reorganized into a new school district. It included three of the Olmsted Township subdistricts and two from Dover Township. The district continued to send older students to Cleveland and Elyria for high school until 1927, when it entered into a contract with North Ridgeville.

A 1914 law created the Cuyahoga County Board of Education, which provided further oversight over all the school districts in the county. But an even more important change for the future of Olmsted schools began about then. Sentiment grew among residents to create one unified school system for both the township and Olmsted Falls. The township's consolidation of its own school system a decade earlier made that more feasible, but another development helped spur interest among village residents for merger. In 1914, the forty-year-old Union School was declared structurally unsafe, causing classes to be moved to the town hall. In 1915, a small, short-term newspaper, the *Olmsted Recorder*, was created solely to promote the consolidation of school districts.

In 1915, fifty Olmsted Falls residents petitioned to dissolve the village's school district and merge it with the Olmsted Township Rural School District. In an April 20 election, fifty village voters favored the proposal and thirty-two opposed it. "The progressive element of the village are more than pleased by the result of the election Tuesday," the *Berea Enterprise* reported. The Olmsted Falls Village Board of Education met for the final time on June 3 and turned over its assets, including a check for $323.07, to the rural district.

One School

The next step was to build a new school. When members of the village and township boards held a joint meeting on May 11, 1915—shortly before the merger—they agreed that a new school should be built. The June 4 edition of the *Berea Enterprise* included an article pitching advantages of school centralization, including:

> *A new modern building, safe—lighting, seating and heating properly designed for the comfort and health of the pupils with proper accommodations for all the pupils of the township, including four-year first class high school.*
>
> *Grounds comprising four or five acres, with room for teaching agriculture properly…and for play grounds.*
>
> *Children living at any distance from the school will be transported between their homes and the school in properly equipped wagons, under the supervision of a competent driver, who will have the necessary authority to preserve perfect order in the wagons.*

There would be a special teacher for music, writing and drawing, and most teachers would have to teach only one grade.

The *Enterprise* concluded, "Larger classes and more interest shown by the pupils, will encourage pupils to go to high school, who could not do it if they had to pay railroad fare or board in Cleveland or Elyria."

On June 8, just days after the establishment of the unified school system, another election was held to consider a $40,000 bond issue to buy land and

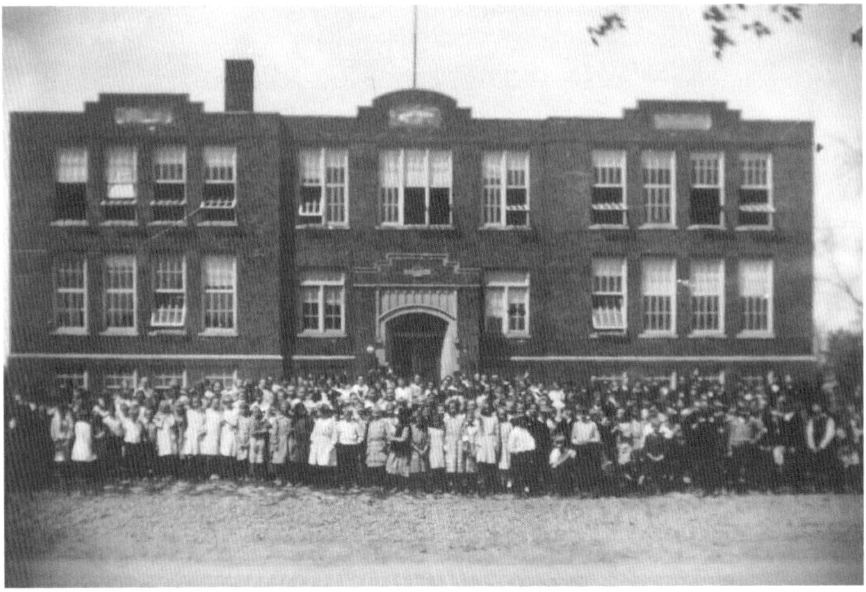

Olmsted built its consolidated school on a site that had been a corn patch amid a large stretch of farmland.

build a school. This time, opponents prevailed with 137 votes against it and 131 for it.

But five months later, the result was different. On November 2, a $65,000 bond issue passed on a 146-138 vote. That resulted in construction of a two-story brick school building at what became the corner of Bagley Road and Mapleway Drive. The school opened in 1916 and served as the district's sole schoolhouse for almost four decades. Through consolidation, the Olmsted district became the first in Cuyahoga County to eliminate use of one-room schools—a rare occasion when Olmsted was ahead of its neighboring communities.

Further in the spirit of educational improvement, the local chapter of the Parent-Teacher Association began in 1917. One of the first projects the PTA took on was to provide hot lunches to students. Although the new school building initially lacked a kitchen, PTA members brought in hot soup and other food.

Busing

The school system transported students to and from all parts of the township and village in "kid wagons"—horse-drawn enclosed wagons with benches along each side. It cost the school board $170 each to buy eight of them, plus $45 a month for each driver and team of horses and $1,000 for barns to store the wagons.

Later, as automobiles took the place of horses, the kid wagons were replaced by farm trucks. Holzworth described one as "a sort of motorized tent with a tarpaulin stretched over a framework and a set of steps from the rear end gate for entrance and exit."

The district eventually replaced the trucks with school buses. Brothers Chester and Bruce Atkinson won the initial contract for the service, using four buses. Their first bus terminal was on Columbia Road. Later, they replaced it with a large garage on Schady Road.

When the unified school district began transporting students, it had a problem with the northeastern corner of the township along Ruple, Spafford and Cedar Point Roads. Not only was it far from the new school, but it also was on the other side of the west branch of the Rocky River

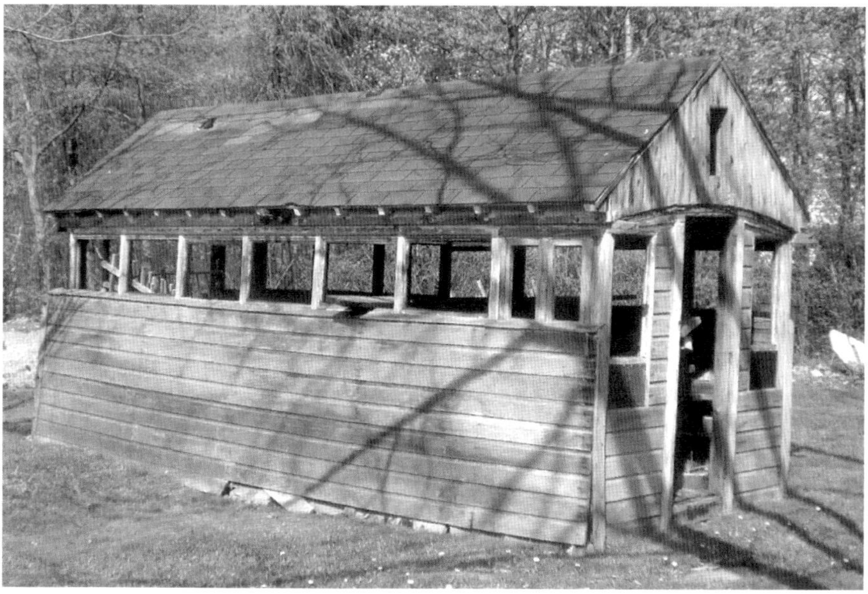

The carriage from a former kid wagon was used later in the township as a doghouse and for storage of wood. *Photo by Bruce Banks.*

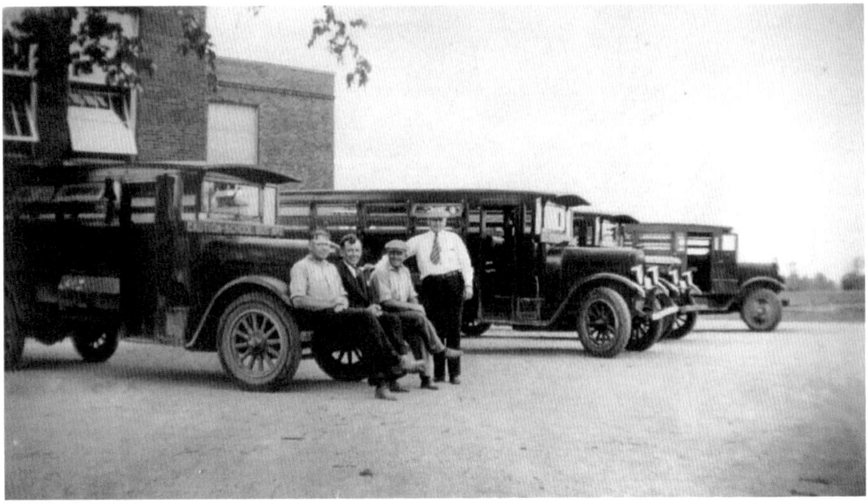

Early in the twentieth century, students went to school in these buses.

and the terrain was hilly. The school board decided it was easier and less expensive to pay tuition for the students to attend schools in Brook Park, which had formed from the northern portion of East Middleburgh Township in 1914. Eventually, that section of Olmsted Township was annexed to Brook Park.

In 1925, the Olmsted Township Rural School District changed its name to the Olmsted Falls School District.

BORDER GROWTH TO BULLDOGS

The district gained territory in 1928 when what was known as the Roth District of Columbia Township was added to the Olmsted Falls district. It remained that way until 1948, when the state school board decided to return to Columbia's school system the section bounded by Columbia and Nichols Roads and the tracks of the New York Central Railroad. Holzworth wrote that the main reason for the change was to eliminate a dangerous railroad crossing for some students attending school in Olmsted Falls. That left a triangular section bounded by Sprague, Mitchell and Root Roads and the railroad tracks within Olmsted's school district.

In 1930, North Olmsted students began attending a new $278,000 high school on land their school board had bought a year earlier along Butternut

Ridge Road. "In a short space of time North Olmsted High equaled the Olmsted Falls High, and then forged rapidly ahead as the North Olmsted population grew," Holzworth wrote.

In 1935, the North Central Association of Colleges and Secondary Schools accepted the Olmsted Falls school as a member, which allowed graduates to be accepted in colleges without taking a special examination. At that time, only 329 of Ohio's 1,442 high schools had such accreditation.

In 1945, Olmsted Falls High School acquired something that has stuck with the school district ever since: a nickname. The school held a contest to determine what to call its sports teams. Sally Geist of the class of 1948 offered the winning entry. Ever since then, Olmsted's teams have been known as the Bulldogs.

Parochial Schools

In 1949, St. Mary's of the Falls reestablished Catholic education in Olmsted Falls. The church had set up a parochial school in 1874, when it bought the old school that was replaced by the Union School and moved it near the church. By that December, an *Advertiser* item noted that "the Catholics have started a school again, so that all classes can be suited as far as educational matters are concerned." This was just a year after the church itself had been moved from the northern end of the central business district to the southern end. But the Catholic school did not last. "The subsequent national financial panic forced the parish to close the school," an essay on St. Mary's church in the 1939 Olmsted Falls Homecoming souvenir program stated. "It has never reopened."

To reopen the school, the church obtained buildings from World War II housing projects in Cleveland, moved them to the church grounds and refurbished them for use as classrooms. The school has continued ever since, although the facilities have been upgraded. Each year, hundreds of children in kindergarten through eighth grade attend St. Mary's school. When they reach high school age, many of them attend Olmsted Falls High School, although some go to Catholic schools in the area, such as St. Edward High School in Lakewood and Magnificat High School in Rocky River.

Booming

Although Olmsted Falls and Olmsted Township grew more slowly than other Cleveland suburbs, growth eventually strained the facilities of Olmsted's school, especially after World War II. In 1948, the school board built an addition with seven elementary classrooms on to the school. At that time, the Atkinsons added a fifth school bus to their fleet.

The public school system in Olmsted Falls incorporated kindergarten into its offerings in 1950. The kindergarten had started in 1944 as private preschool classes held on the upper floor of the town hall.

The 1948 addition to the 1916 school failed to handle the community's growth for very long. In 1953, the school board decided to build a new elementary school directly west of the existing school. It opened in September 1954 as Falls Elementary School. Additions were built on to it in 1955 and 1957.

Still growing with the baby boom, the district opened Fitch Elementary School in September 1958 and gave it a small addition in 1961. That school was still new when yet another school, Lenox Elementary, opened just west of Falls Elementary in January 1961.

But even as the community welcomed new buildings, it let an old one go. The Union Schoolhouse on the Village Green had not been used as a school for decades. The building had been neglected and vandalized. In 1960, it was torn down. Many people hated to see it go and often expressed regret later about not saving it.

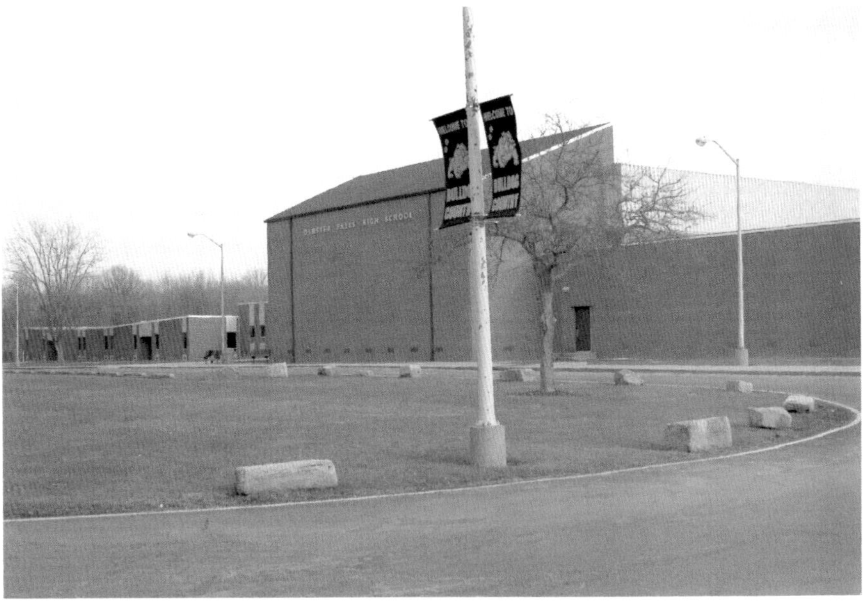

When Olmsted Falls High School opened in 1968, it was the district's first new school for ninth through twelfth graders in fifty-two years. *Photo by Jim Wallace.*

During the next few years, school board members and district residents turned their attention to the needs of the older students. By 1965, they developed plans to build a new high school. The board acquired a forty-seven-acre site on Bagley Road west of Fitch Road in Olmsted Township. When the new high school opened in September 1968, the old 1916 school became a middle school for grades six through eight. Other schools also were realigned. Fitch became a school for kindergarten through fourth grade. All the fifth-graders went to Falls Elementary.

Thus, within fifteen years, the Olmsted Falls School District went from having just one school to operating four schools. For two years, football games were still played on the old high school field. The new high school field opened in 1970.

Togetherness

In the 1970s, the merger of Olmsted Falls and West View allowed Olmsted Falls to become a city. The school district then had the opportunity to become Olmsted Falls City School District on July 1, 1975. It was more than a slight name change. Under Ohio law, a city school district is autonomous, while a local school district comes under the jurisdiction of the county school board.

In the 1970s, the Olmsted Falls district joined neighboring districts in the establishment of a joint vocational district. That led to the 1975 opening of Polaris Career Center in Middleburg Heights to train high school juniors and seniors in technical career-oriented subjects. From then on, some Olmsted students' high school education included classes at both Olmsted Falls High School and Polaris. The joint vocational district includes the Berea, Brooklyn, Fairview Park, North Olmsted and Strongsville districts, in addition to Olmsted Falls. Polaris also offers adult education classes.

Building along Bagley

The next big growth spurt for the Olmsted Falls City School District came in the 1990s. Thanks to a successful bond issue in the November 1990 election, $8.2 million in construction and renovation work at the elementary-level schools was completed in 1992. It included a 28,000-square-foot addition linking Falls and Lenox Elementaries. The combined building was renamed Falls-Lenox Primary School. Meanwhile, the district added 17,500 square feet to Fitch Elementary School and renamed it Fitch Intermediate School. Before the changes, Lenox and Fitch housed kindergarteners through third graders, and Falls housed fourth and fifth graders. After construction, kindergarten and first-grade students went to the Falls section of the combined school, second and third graders went to the Lenox side and fourth and fifth graders went to Fitch.

But while the elementary students were getting new facilities, the facilities for middle school students in the old 1916 building were wearing out. In 1993, the school system closed part of the building because of health and safety problems. Classes that had been held in the basement were moved into three trailers behind the school. The board of education decided the school would have to close in 1996.

A strong campaign persuaded voters in November 1994 to approve a $10 million bond issue to build a new school, as well as a 2.9-mill incremental operating levy. By passing the bond issue then, the district qualified for $7 million from a state building assistance program. The incremental operating levy was notable because it was the first time a school district in Cuyahoga County had tried that funding method. Unlike a standard levy, in which a district gets the full millage from the start, the amount from an incremental levy builds up in steps over two or more years.

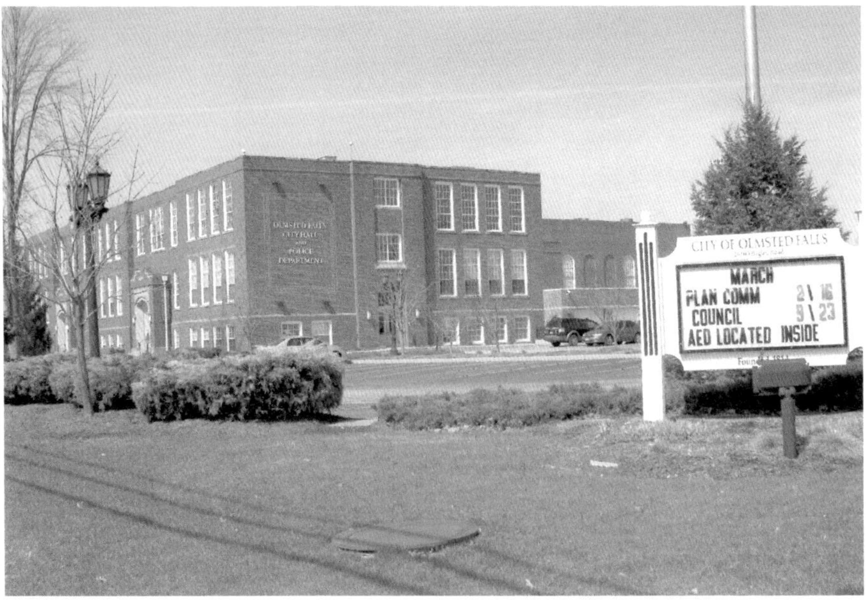

The 1916 school became city hall. *Photo by Jim Wallace.*

In November 1996, the new 123,140-square-foot Olmsted Falls Middle School, about twice as big as 1916 school, opened on sixty-three acres of land on Bagley Road a short distance west of the high school. It was a $15 million project with 45 percent paid by the state.

About that same time, ten classrooms, a gymnasium and a wrestling room were added to the high school. The kitchen, library-media center, auditorium and guidance offices also were renovated.

There was much discussion about what to do with the old 1916 school building. Moving the public library into it—or building a new library at that site—was one proposal. At one time, the school board was determined to tear the building down. But by March 1997, the school board reached agreement to sell it to FirstNorth Development Corp. of Cleveland for $225,000. Subsequently, the developer refurbished the building to serve three new purposes. The western end became a day-care center. The main, and oldest, portion became Olmsted Falls City Hall. The old gym and cafeteria became a community center.

Winning and Losing

Meanwhile, the district's students thrived. Athletically, the Bulldogs fielded strong teams that were contenders for Southwestern Conference championships. Olmsted students also performed well academically. High school students had scores higher than state and national averages on college admission tests, the ACT and the SAT. In 1998, the U.S. Department of Education chose Olmsted Falls High School as a Blue Ribbon School, one of just 14 in Ohio and 167 nationwide.

Despite such achievements, the district had trouble passing operating levies. In November 1998, residents rejected a 9.8-mill incremental operating levy by a vote of 3,549 to 3,025. The defeat came despite school officials' warning that they would have to borrow money to pay bills and eliminate busing for many students. In January 1999, high school students had to find their own way to school. The district also cut adult education, staff instruction and other expenses to reduce spending by $1.5 million.

In February 1999, the district tried again with a 12.9-mill continuing operating levy. School officials warned that its failure would lead to cutting busing for all students within two miles of school, eliminating the jobs of forty-five teachers and other employees and dropping several academic courses and all extracurricular activities. This time, the levy passed on a vote of 2,395 to

2,198. The district still had to borrow about $2 million from the state just to get through 1999 because levy revenues did not start coming in until 2000.

Voters could not have realized at the time that if the levy had failed and extracurricular activities had been eliminated, Olmsted Falls High School would have been denied its greatest athletic achievement ever. In 2000, the Bulldogs won the Ohio High School Athletic Association's state football championship. Under Coach Jim Ryan, Olmsted Falls defeated Piqua 21–0 in the championship game played in Massillon. It was all the more remarkable for many alumni, who remembered numerous years when Olmsted Falls High School suffered from being the smallest school in the Southwestern Conference. Steady population growth toward the end of the century helped overcome that size difference.

In 2005, the football stadium at the high school received a $720,000 upgrade, including new homestands, a press box and a better sound system. The Olmsted Falls Endowment and Alumni Association raised the funds for the improvements. Because of major donations from Amelia and Clara Harding and the Shaker family, the stadium was renamed Charles A. Harding Memorial Stadium with the Robert Shaker/Class of 1972 Press Box. Bob Shaker died of cancer in 1999.

In May 2007, district voters approved a bond issue to build a $16 million, eighty-three-thousand-square-foot intermediate school next to the middle school. It opened for fourth and fifth graders in August 2009. Fitch Intermediate Center was renovated to become the Olmsted Falls Early Childhood Center with classrooms devoted to preschool and kindergarten classes.

In 2008, Olmsted Falls girls reached the athletic pinnacle when the varsity volleyball team won a state championship. In addition to that and other accomplishments by athletes wearing the high school's blue and gold, Olmsted students kept up the district's high standards for academic performance. The Ohio Department of Education rated the school system among the state's High-Performing Districts for 2000–01 and every year since then (as of this writing). In the early years of the twenty-first century, more than three-quarters of high school graduates went on to college or university education.

School officials credited much of that success to having a stable teaching force in which about two-thirds of the teachers had master's degrees. At the high school level, all the teachers were certified in the subjects they taught, a status not found in all school districts. The district also boasted about being the first in the county to have Internet access in every classroom. These achievements occurred despite the school system's frugality; per-pupil spending was lower than three-quarters of the thirty-one school districts in Cuyahoga County.

Despite that strong record, the school system once again struggled to persuade voters to approve a new operating levy. A combination property tax/income tax in November 2008 and a traditional 9.9-mill levy in February 2009 each failed by a 2-1 ratio. The February loss resulted in the elimination of busing for high school students at the beginning of the 2009–10 school year. The school board warned that busing for kindergarteners through eighth graders would be eliminated if the next levy failed. The board also warned that lack of a new levy would result in elimination of middle school sports and other extracurricular activities and eventually all high school extracurricular activities, including sports, as well as staff cutbacks. Despite the warnings, a 6.4-mill levy for about $3.5 million for annual operating expenses failed in November 2009. But the margin was only 176 out of 9,174 votes cast—a better showing than the two previous levy attempts.

The school system had the misfortune of seeking a tax levy during the nation's deepest recession since the 1930s. The district already had been hindered by having higher residential tax rates than most neighboring communities because of a paucity of commercial and industrial property. For the 2009 tax year, an Olmsted Falls City School district resident had to pay $1,392 for every $100,000 of property value. Among western Cuyahoga County districts, that was lower than the $1,731 in Fairview Park and $1,432 in Bay Village. But it was higher than the $1,366 in North Olmsted, $1,296 in Rocky River, $1,236 in Strongsville, $1,184 in Berea and $1,007 in Westlake. Rates were much lower in neighboring districts in Lorain County: $989 in Columbia Township and $878 in North Ridgeville.

The school board tried again in February 2010 with an 8.7-mill levy that would cost $266 a year for each $100,000 of property value. This time, the levy issue succeeded with a vote of 4,374 to 3,644. The district gradually restored busing and other services that had been cut, even though money from the levy was not due to come in until 2011. School officials noted that the number of students in the system had increased more than 28 percent since voters had last approved an operating levy eleven years earlier.

SALOON WARS

Olmsted Falls has had a reputation as a tranquil community throughout its history, but that did not stop it from being a battleground. For decades, it was the scene of skirmishes between supporters of saloons and those who advocated temperance or prohibition. Those battles sometimes spilled over into the surrounding township.

It is not recorded when the first saloon opened, but by the 1870s, there were several in and around the village, as well as an active temperance movement opposed to them. West View acquired its first saloon late in 1874 that soon was reported to be going "full blast." But people along Butternut Ridge boasted about being "cursed with neither Billiard saloon, Beer hall nor Rum hole."

Throughout the 1870s and 1880s, numerous items about activities of temperance groups and prohibition advocates ran in the *Advertiser*, which took a firm editorial stand against saloons. Although Olmsted voters strongly supported Republican candidates over Democrats, it was not unusual for candidates on the third-party Prohibition ticket to get some votes.

One notable effort against alcohol occurred on Friday afternoon, March 27, 1874, when a committee from the Women's Temperance League went to visit businesses in Olmsted Falls that sold alcoholic drinks. First, they went to a saloon, where they interrupted a game of billiards and told the proprietor they wanted him to get out of the saloon business. He replied that he would give it up if they were prepared to buy him out. "He acknowledged that it was not a pleasant business, but he must do something to support his family," the *Advertiser* reported.

When the ladies called on the store of Thomas Pollard, he was not in. So they moved on to the hotel, where proprietor Loren Fitch told them he kept "a respectable business" and that he could not operate a hotel without a bar to sell ale to travelers. Finally, the women went to the drugstore of Newton Loomis, who was suspected of having sold liquor to people who were in the habit of getting intoxicated. That might have happened, he acknowledged, but it was unintentional, and he promised to be more careful in the future. "The ladies left scarcely daring to hope that they had accomplished any good, but with the satisfaction that they had added their mite [*sic*] to the labors of the women who are engaged in this good work," the newspaper reported.

Short Arm of the Law

In 1874, residents persuaded the Olmsted Falls Council to pass the McConnellsville Ordinance, which was named after a law adopted in 1869 in McConnellsville, Ohio. That ordinance prohibited establishments from selling beer and other alcoholic drinks for consumption on the premises. It failed to have the effect its promoters expected.

"Beer drinkers now go to the saloon and buy their beer by the quart, borrow the measure and a glass, and go out on the sidewalk and drink," the *Advertiser* reported in May 1874. It further said that "unless there is some way to put a stop to it, the liquor traffic will be more of a nuisance than it was before the passage of the McConnellsville Ordinance." Pleas for the council to repeal the ordinance went unheeded for several months, and it is not clear when action was ever taken on that request.

In March 1876, the council passed a new ordinance to close "all billiard saloons and places where games of chance are played" from 9:30 p.m. until 6:00 a.m. But it did not seem to put a damper on such businesses. When one Olmsted Falls resident rented a place for a new saloon in February 1877, the *Advertiser* reported, "We have now no less than seven places where intoxicating liquors are sold in some shape." Yet another was reported to be opening on the west side of Plum Creek in July 1878. In August 1879, the council had a raucous debate when neighbors of saloons complained "that a noisy crowd was at the saloons late at night—sometimes all night, Sundays included." The council adjourned without taking action. But that September, members voted five to one in favor of a new ordinance requiring saloons to close between 9:30 p.m. and 6:00 a.m. and on Saturday from 10:00 p.m. until 6:00 a.m. on Monday.

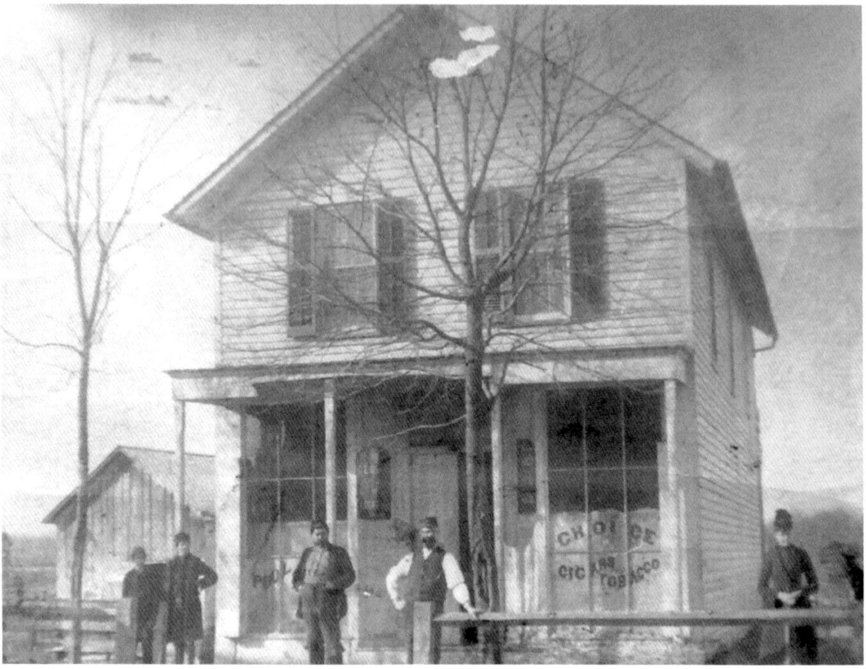

A pool hall was added later to this saloon, which is now occupied by the Olde Wine Cellar.

Passing such ordinances was not the same as enforcing them. In October 1882, council members felt compelled to reaffirm their intention of enforcing an ordinance that, by then, called for saloons to close by 9:00 p.m. "The saloons in question have abused all moral and legal rights of society, keeping open at all hours of the night, and it is reported the state law regarding the selling of intoxicating liquor to minors has been violated in some instances," the *Advertiser* reported. "It is a b-a-d business boys."

It's not clear what happened to that ordinance, but in October 1885, the council passed another ordinance calling for the saloons to close at 9:30 p.m. every day, except Saturday, when they could stay open until 10:00 p.m. This time, it was noted, "Marshal Taylor is on deck every night to ring the curfew and to extinguish the lights if the law is not immediately complied with." Yet, once again, the ordinance was not heeded, and in May 1886, it was brought to the council's attention that "the busy Olmsted officers had forgot to notify the keepers of such place."

In July 1886, one citizen, Frank Lay, sued William Wagner, who ran the saloon later owned by Herman Fenderbosch, for violating the closing ordinance. But the case was dismissed on grounds of insufficient evidence. A newspaper reporter expressed concern that saloonkeepers would be emboldened by that result: "Brawling and indecent language is indulged in nearly every day on the main street to the thorough disgust of the people, who feel they can do nothing other than tolerate it."

A Test of Will—Voters versus Drinkers

It was also in 1886 that the Ohio General Assembly offered to help communities curtail drinking problems by passing the Dow Law. This law permitted taxing saloon owners $200 a year and regulating alcohol trafficking throughout Ohio. It also gave local governments the option of restricting or prohibiting sale of alcohol within their borders. The prohibitionists in Olmsted Falls tried as early as July that year to get the council to exercise that local option clause. They held enthusiastic, well-attended meetings in the town hall and in a grove north of the village to urge action. The village council set a referendum for August 13. To the disappointment of prohibitionists, the majority favored allowing the saloons to stay open, or as the *Advertiser* put it, "to continue their nefarious and damnable business of robbery, murder, pauper-making, heartbreaking, soul-destroying, tax producing and law-defying."

In 1888, the antisaloon people decided to try to get the township voted dry before making another attempt in the village. The idea was to remove the argument that Olmsted Falls was so small that if saloons were prohibited within village limits, they would merely "move a few rods" into the township and keep doing business. That method worked. The township voted against saloons in May; in June, village residents voted 53 to 41 for going dry. The village council then passed an ordinance for all the saloons in town to close by August 1. On August 3, the *Advertiser* ran an obituary for the saloons but also noted that the proprietors "have not taken down their signs. Some of them will probably run strictly temperance places selling nothing but light drinks." That September, the Prohibition Convention of Cuyahoga County met in Olmsted Falls with about 150 people in attendance.

But the new law was not enough to put saloons out of business. Proprietors kept them going under the guise of selling only nonalcoholic drinks. At least one saloonkeeper was fined $25.00 and costs for violating the law in 1889. Also that year, two other saloon operators, Herman Fenderbosch and Joseph Nickels, sued the county treasurer to prevent him from collecting $246.84 and $205.70, respectively, for the Dow Law tax. They contended that they

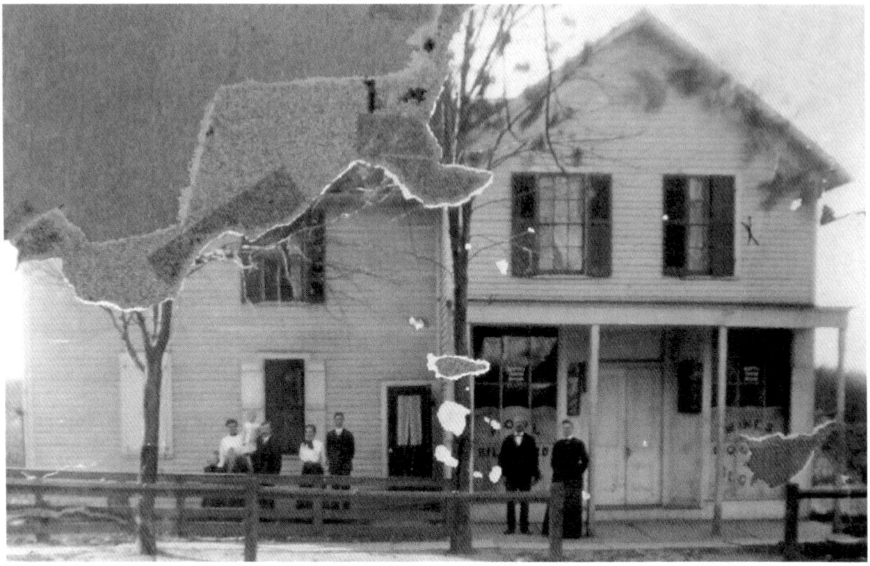

Herman Fenderbosch bought this saloon in the 1880s.

had paid the tax in full up to the time they quit the saloon business. But a different story came out in court. Several witnesses in the hearing in the Nickels case "testified that they drank both beer and whisky" at his saloon. The judge ruled in favor of the treasurer. A few weeks later, it was reported that Nickels had "closed his billiard room, for want of business, and gone west prospecting for a short time."

In December 1890, the *Cleveland Leader* reported in an article about Olmsted Falls: "The saloons in this place are all running openly doing a so-called hop tea business, but just as many drunken men are seen on the streets as when the stuff was called by its right name."

WETTER WAYS

In April 1891, village residents voted in a "wet" council, whose members took action as soon as they were sworn in. "One of their first acts was to repeal the local option law passed two or three years ago, but which has been feebly enforced," the *Advertiser* reported. That May, it was noted that Olmsted Falls had four saloons that together paid annual Dow Law taxes of $1,000, with two-thirds of that going to the village.

In April 1895, the township also reversed itself and voted to go wet again by a margin of just twenty-two. It was speculated that West View area residents who wanted to drink legally were motivated to vote, while other township residents were less motivated or content to "let West View do her own voting."

Saloon foes tried again in April 1897 with another local option election in the township. "We hope the township will redeem itself," the Olmsted Falls correspondent for the *Advertiser* wrote.

"Will North Olmsted do its duty next Monday and get out a full vote?" the Butternut Ridge correspondent asked. "There is a big anti-saloon vote in this part of the township, and every vote is needed next Monday. Have the township 'dry' by outlawing the saloon."

Likewise, the West View correspondent wrote that members of the West View chapter of the Woman's Christian Temperance Union

> *are greatly interested in temperance agitation just now. Next Monday the township vote*[s] *on the saloon question again, and they want every temperance vote at West View to be cast against the saloon. Let no one stay at home; let every temperance worker be as active as the saloon element, and the result will be in our favor.*

However, the "saloon element" again prevailed. After all of its buildup prior to the election, the *Advertiser* gave just one line to the result the following week: "The township went wet by forty-three majority."

Drier Days

In 1908, the dry side prevailed in the village. A praise service was soon held at the Methodist church, but many on the losing side were reported to be disgruntled. "Dire threats are made as to what will be done, but so far nothing has happened out of the ordinary," the *Advertiser* reported. "It is said that the boycott is to be used. Some people may find that two can play at that game."

Several months later, in November 1908, the township also went dry on a vote of 109 to 97. In 1914, an attempt to permit saloons again in the village failed on a vote of 87 to 49.

When Prohibition went into effect nationally in 1920, it put an end to the seesaw battle of local option elections in Olmsted Falls and Olmsted

Township. That's not to say it ended drinking; the alcohol business merely went underground until Prohibition was repealed in 1933.

Even after repeal, no one attempted to sell alcoholic drinks in Olmsted Falls for at least another five years. But a proposal for a nightclub in town late in 1938 drove 206 citizens, representing about two-thirds of the voters in the village, to sign a petition calling for a local option election. In the subsequent election in February 1939, voters were very thorough. They voted on five questions:

1) Shall the sale of any intoxicating liquor be permitted?
2) Shall the sale of wine by the package for consumption off the premises be sold or permitted?
3) Shall the sale of wine for consumption on and off the premises where sold be permitted?
4) Shall the sale of spirituous liquors by the glass be permitted?
5) Shall state liquor stores be permitted?

In each case, the number of yes votes ranged from 67 to 69 while the no votes ranged from 228 to 230. That firmly established Olmsted Falls as a dry town for many years. However, village residents did not have to go far for a drink; by then, bars already had been established in West View and Olmsted Township.

The "dryness" of Olmsted Falls later became an issue in attempts to annex the township to the village. For example, during one attempt in 1968, township trustee William Gilligan wondered what would happen to the township's taverns if it became part of Olmsted Falls. Council president Charles Wright responded that the Falls would remain dry and what was the township would remain wet until voters could decide the issue in 1970. However, the annexation didn't happen, so the issue was moot. After Olmsted Falls and West View merged in 1971, the new municipality initially kept things the same: the former West View remained wet, and the rest of the town remained dry.

A ROAD BY ANY OTHER NAME

Many American communities have Main Streets, but most of them live up to their names. In Olmsted Falls, MAIN STREET is only two blocks long, and neither end is a through street, except for pedestrians who can stroll across the covered bridge over Plum Creek.

Another Olmsted oddity is Nobottom Road. Surely, it's unlikely that any other community would have a road with such a name—except, of course, Berea, which shares that distinction with Olmsted Falls and Olmsted Township.

Those are a couple of curiosities about roadway names in Olmsted, but most of the long-standing roads and streets around the Falls and the township came by their names in more apparent and standard ways. Most commonly, roads were named after the early settlers who lived along them:

STEARNS ROAD for the Stearns family, who arrived from Vermont in 1815.
FITCH ROAD for the Fitch family, who arrived from Connecticut in 1831.
SCHADY ROAD for German immigrant Henry Schady and his wife, Clara.
COOK ROAD for Caleb Cook, who moved there from Connecticut in 1827.
USHER ROAD for Watrous Usher, who moved to Olmsted (then Lenox) in 1820.
JENNINGS ROAD for the Jennings family, who came to Olmsted in 1863.
SPRAGUE ROAD for the Sprague family.
BRONSON ROAD for the Bronson family.
LEWIS ROAD for the Lewis family, although it once was called Seminary Road for the seminary located there. That seminary building was moved across Rocky River and became the Grand Pacific Hotel.

Less obvious is JOHN ROAD, which was named after John Hall, who had a farm along it. In the twentieth century, his farm became Homelinks Golf Course and, later, the Links golf course and the Renaissance.

FERNHALL ROAD, an unpaved, dead-end road off of THORNBROOK ROAD, which is off of John Road, was named for John Hall's wife, Fern. The houses along Fernhall and Thornbrook were built in the 1950s.

RIVER ROAD is obviously named because it runs on the ridge parallel to the west branch of the Rocky River, but it didn't always have that name. In the early 1800s, it was called Bradford Road after the Bradford family, who moved there in 1820. Later, it became River Street before taking its current name, River Road. Some of the oldest homes in Olmsted Falls are located along River Road.

Other streets also have names that refer to their locations:

WATER STREET runs over the Rocky River.

MILL STREET once ran down past Damp's Mill east of Columbia Road. It now runs only west of Columbia.

ORCHARD STREET apparently once was located next to an Orchard.

NORTH DEPOT STREET was near the train depot. It used to be paired with SOUTH DEPOT STREET, where the depot is located, but South Depot was renamed GARFIELD STREET.

COLUMBIA ROAD, once called Columbia Street, got its name because it ran south from Olmsted Falls to Columbia Township. At one time, Columbia Street was an almost straight street that included what is now Main Street, with its northern end at Water Street. The northern part of what is now Columbia Road, beginning at the intersection of what is now Main Street, was called Main Street. Thus, the Main Street of that time was more of a "main street" than the current Main Street.

Several streets changed names over the years. What is now BAGLEY ROAD had a few different names. During the 1800s, the section west of Olmsted Falls was called Dutch Road because of settlers of Dutch origin. (SCHADY ROAD also was called Second Dutch Road.) HAMLIN STREET was the portion within the village of Olmsted Falls. It was named after E.S. Hamlin, a lawyer from Lorain County who served in the state legislature. He laid out many of the streets in Olmsted Falls. IRISH ROAD was the section that opened in 1871 connecting Olmsted Falls and Berea. It got its name from the Irish residents on each end. One on the Olmsted end, James Hickey, had the honor of driving the first team of horses over

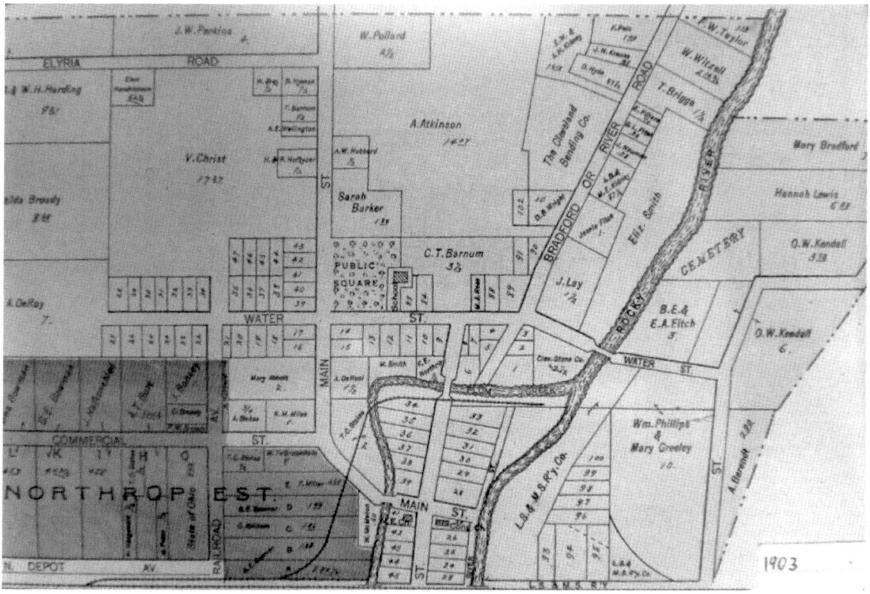

On this 1903 map, the northern part of Columbia Road was still called Main Street. The current Main Street was still part of Columbia Street. Elm Street was then Commercial Street, Brookside Drive was Railroad Avenue and Cook Road was Elyria Road.

the road when it opened. The whole roadway, passing through several communities, eventually took on the name Berea gave it: Bagley for Abijah Bagley, who managed a successful farm there.

Another street that changed names is Mapleway Drive. It once was called Division Street.

How Nobottom Road got its name is not clear. Perhaps it was because the road originally crossed the Rocky River before a bridge collapsed. Perhaps it was because the mud on the road was so soggy in the spring that it seemed the road had no bottom. Why Nobottom? Nobody really knows.

BIBLIOGRAPHY

Berea Advertiser, 1879–1909.

Berea Enterprise, 1898–1955.

Berea News, 1924–1967.

Bonsey, Charles. Personal interview, March 26, 1982.

Cleveland Plain Dealer, 1926–1972.

Cuyahoga Republican and Advertiser, 1877.

Grindstone City Advertiser, 1869–1877.

Hansen, Gayle. Presentation to Historical Society of Olmsted Falls, November 16, 2009.

Hill, Dan. Chestnut Grove Cemetery tour, August 19, 2007.

Holzworth, Walter F. *Township 6, Range 15: Historical Story: Olmsted Township, Villages of Olmsted Falls, North Olmsted, West View.* N.p., 1966.

Johnson, Crisfield. *History of Cuyahoga County, Ohio; Part Third: The Townships.* N.p.: D.W. Ensign & Co., 1879.

[The] *News*, 1967–1969.

News Sun, 1970–2009.

Offenberg, Bernice. *Over the Years in Olmsted, Township 6, Range 15.* N.p., 1964.

Republican and Advertiser, 1877–1879.

Roberts, Les. *King of the Holly Hop.* Cleveland, OH: Gray & Company, 2008.

Segal, Eugene. "Howdy Neighbor: Olmsted Falls." *Cleveland Press*, April 19, 1941.

Thomas, Dale. *North Olmsted.* Charleston, SC: Arcadia Publishing, 2008.

Weitzel, Lura. Personal interview, January 30, 1983.

Williams, Clint. Personal interview, August 16, 2004.

INDEX

L

M

N

O

P

Q

R

S

T

V

W

Z

ABOUT THE AUTHORS

Jim Wallace is the senior counsel for public relations for TSG Consulting, Charleston, West Virginia. He grew up in Olmsted Township, where his co-author, physicist and local historian Bruce Banks, currently resides. They are both members of the Historical Society of Olmsted Falls. Mr. Banks has presented illustrated lectures for more than twenty-five years on the history of Olmsted Falls and Olmsted Township.

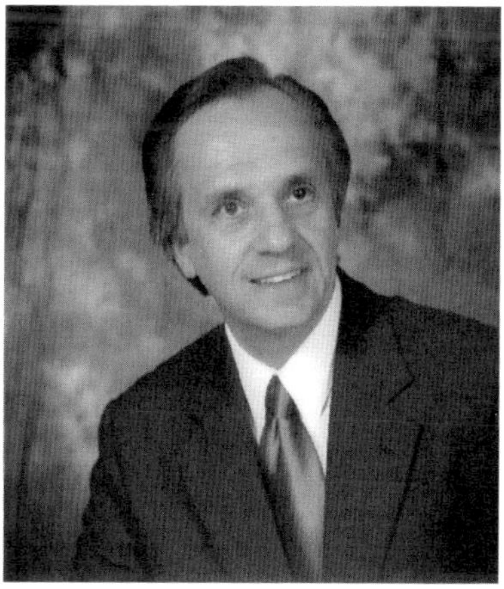

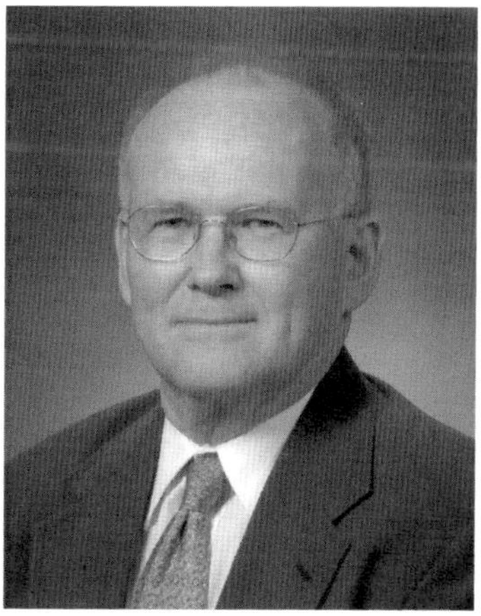